W9-CJT-011

Date D

Borderlines

Borderlines

What Canadians and Americans
Should – But Don't – Know About
Each Other . . . a Witty, Punchy
and Personal Look

Roger Sauvé

McGraw-Hill Ryerson
Toronto Montreal

BORDERLINES
What Canadians and Americans Should – But Don't – Know
About Each Other... A Witty, Punchy and Personal Look

First published in 1994 by
McGraw-Hill Ryerson Limited
300 Water Street
Whitby, Ontario, Canada
L1N 9B6

1 2 3 4 5 6 7 8 9 0 T R I 3 2 1 0 8 7 6 5 4

Canadian Cataloguing in Publication Data

Sauvé, Roger
    Borderlines

ISBN 0-07-551857-0

1. Canada – Social conditions – 1971 –   .*
2. Canada – Economic conditions – 1991 –   .*
3. United States – Social conditions – 1980 –   .*
4. United States – Economic conditions – 1981 –   .*
I. Title.

FC97.S38 1994   971.064'7   C94–931657–1
F1021.2.S38 1994

Permission to reprint statistics from "Portrait of Two Nations" published in *Maclean's* (July 3, 1989) is gratefully acknowledged.

Publisher: Donald S. Broad
Cover design: Dianna Little
Text design: Dave Hader/ Studio Conceptions
Copy editor: David McCabe
Editorial services provided by Word Guild, Markham, Ontario

Printed in Canada

DEDICATION AND THANKS

This book is dedicated to the many people who help give my life meaning, happiness, fulfilment, growth and stability.

Family members include Rosabelle and Adélard, Bonnie, Roxanne and Rob and baby Stephanie, Eric, Jeff and Kerry, Marcie and Jason, Sheree and Ed, Inez, my brothers and sisters Maurice, Hervé, Marie, Eileen, Gérald, and their families.

Thanks also to Marsha, Nadine, Paul, Bob, Laurie, Ken, Diana, Shannon, Debbie and other workplace professionals who often took the time to listen to the "latest" findings.

I want to thank the many people who collected the raw numbers behind this book about real Canadians and Americans, especially Statistics Canada, contributors to the Statistical Abstracts of the United States, and polsters.

Thanks also to editors Don Loney and David McCabe.

CONTENTS

GROWING UP CANADIAN

I love Canada and I like the United States.

Like the majority of Canadians, I was raised within a relatively short driving distance to the Canada-United States border and have always seen the U.S. as that nice but "foreign" country just next door. From about the age of six and throughout my teens, crossing the bridge "to the States" was an awesome experience for me. Sometimes we would drive over the bridge and come right back just to say we had been to another country. For me, the return trip was always more emotional because I felt proud to be a Canadian. Somehow, Canada was always a nicer and more comfortable place...that was where I felt at home. As I hit 50, I still feel this way, although I love to travel all over the United States and meet American people.

Some of my first memories of the United States relate to music on the radio. I especially remember listening to western music on WWBA—"direct from Wheeling, West Virginia"—and broadcasts of rock and roll music from various cities in New York State. This music was intertwined with what I heard over English and French stations in Canada. A bit later, I remember watching television programs from both sides of the border. Somehow, it all seemed to fit together.

In high school, I began to believe that those Americans were really not as nice as they seemed. This was in part stimulated by listening to a fiery nationalistic speech delivered in the town hall by then-Prime Minister John Diefenbaker. I can still feel the surge of pride in being Canadian that his speech awakened in me. The Americans were taking us over economically and culturally, and we needed to protect ourselves. Those Yanks were no longer my friends. They knew little about Canada and they didn't seem to care.

These early feelings of anti-Americanism made me feel more Canadian. It still seems to have the same effect on me today. My anti-Americanism no longer surfaces as often as it did, even if Americans still don't know much about Canada and still do not seem to care. My love for Canada is now based on the fact that we are Canadian and our country is different from any other nation I know...and I love it.

Through the years, my feelings relative to the United States have wavered from warmth, to pride in their achievements, to envy, and to contempt. To this day, my feelings for the United States are marked by wide swings. I have mixed feelings...I believe that it is through "feelings" that I say that I would rather be a Canadian than an American. I feel and act like a Canadian and not an American.

In my mind and heart, something has changed over the years. More and more, I see the United States as being made up of real people rather than being merely a country. Like Canadians, I like some of them and can live very well without others. This conclusion has been enriched by visiting most of Canada and at least two-thirds of the 50 states.

This personal feeling is the main reason why I decided to write this book. I wanted to see how the average Canadian really compared with the average American. As a numbers person, I made sure that all my comparisons were measurable. The comparisons I have made are mostly related to what average people are interested in as they live their lives. Readers on both sides of the border should be able to see themselves on most pages throughout this book.

Borderlines is an extension of my first book, *Canadian People Patterns,* which examined how the average Canadian was changing over the past few decades. I could have written an "American People Patterns" which might have sold more copies in the United States, but it would not have provided direct quantifiable comparisons of Canadians and Americans. This new book had to help Canadians and Americans to see themselves more clearly. I know that Canadians like to compare themselves to Americans; favourable comparisons make us feel more Canadian.

The topics covered are relatively uncomplicated, non-academic and mostly descriptive, and they are all measurable and as conceptually compatible as possible. All dollar estimates are in Canadian dollars converted at a $1.25 or 80 cent exchange rate for all years. Any exceptions are noted.

The one-page write-ups provide a few answers to the many questions you will ask yourself as you read this book. It is my hope that you will seek your own answers to those questions which are not answered.

I begin each chapter with my personal reflections about what the theme of that chapter means for me; you may be tempted to do the same. How do the comparisons make you feel about being Canadian or American?

This book is the result of a labour of love—I love to self-discover, I love to build new frameworks to look at my life, I love to dig deep enough to challenge some of my basic beliefs, and I love to challenge others to do the same. This book may help you to take a really honest look at yourself as an individual Canadian or an individual American.

WHEN AND HOW I WROTE THIS BOOK

Writing is one of those things I like to do in my spare time. It ranks up there with my enjoyment of family, of playing racquetball, of driving around in my convertible or my motorcycle, and of listening to country music. The majority of this book was written during my extended holiday during the summer and finalized on weekends, with music playing in the background.

The one-page comparisons are written in a style that I like to call short-and-punchy. "Just give 'em the facts" and then let the reader decide what they mean for them. Do you like what the facts say? Do they make you angry? Is there a personal "and so what do I do now" feeling for you? Does the material tell you something about yourself? Does it make you want to get involved? Do the facts make you feel more or less proud of being a Canadian or an American?

The introduction to each chapter attempts to trace some of the questions, introspections and feelings I went through as I collected and assembled the data and wrote up the key findings. The personal stuff was actually the toughest part of writing this book; I had to dig deeper and get beyond the numbers to find personal meaning. For me, this book was a journey of professional and personal discovery. There are a lot of numbers, tables and charts in this book, but it is not a book about statistics—it is a book about the lives of average Canadians and Americans. It is a book about *you.*

The professional findings and how they are presented reflect my work and personal experience. I have spent many of my working years looking for and tracking the general trends in Canada, the United States, and rest of the world. Over the years, I have gradually expanded my scope of examination. I did this by working for eight different organizations in a cross-section of private and public sectors, through teaching and private consulting, and in writing for newspapers and magazines.

I took my master's degree in economics at the University of Ottawa in the mid-1960s. At university, the definition of economics that most attracted me was "the study of people in the everyday business of life." In actual fact, I have found that, as an economist, I practised a much narrower view of economics that emphasised short-term trends in interest rates, exchange rates, quarterly output growth, trade balances, leading economic indicators, industry trends and political stability.

I broadened my content and time horizon by moving into market research. This was the beginning of my professional interest in peoples and how they compare. Much of the emphasis in market research is on finding differences in what people think and do, and how these differences can be used to find markets for old or new products or services.

Demographics was a natural extension from market research. Demography is the study of people and how they change over time. It examines how people evolve over longer time horizons in terms of age, sex, marital status, education, race, language, incomes, wealth and lifestyles, and many other characteristics that help define us as a society. For me, it is the study of people as they are born, live and die. It examines people in their "everyday business of life." This definition is close to what I had originally thought economics was supposed to be all about.

I have made one more step in my professional journey. I now call myself a Futurist. As a Futurist, I look at the future and am concerned with longer-term trends and alternate scenarios of uncertain futures. Futurists are typically involved in several disciplines and get a "big picture" view of the world. I now reluctantly accept the fact that the future cannot be forecast with any degree of accuracy and that the future will most likely be marked by discontinuous rather than predictable change.

The inherent uncertainty of our futures reaffirmed my belief that more of the responsibility for managing my own future—and yours—should be in the hands of us as individuals rather than up to the organizations and governments that surround us. Governments still have a very important role to play in levelling the field so that we all, rich and poor, a majority or a minority, can have a hope of success in our personal ventures. But, it is up to each one of us to do all we can to assure that we have the mindset and tools to survive and prosper in a very uncertain world. Hopefully, this book will help other people to understand their world better and to take more personal responsibility for themselves and others.

Some people might think that I can't hold a job...rather, I believe I can't stand still because I am looking for new excitement and personal challenges in what I study. Writing this book provided some of this excitement and challenge. Reading and enjoying this book, I hope, will do the same for you.

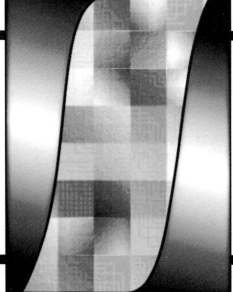

P A R T   1

LAYING
OUT
THE
CHALLENGE

ERASING AN "OLD TAPE"

*H*ow do you compare the people of two countries?

What topics could be covered or, more precisely, what topics can be covered, competently? Should just a few themes be addressed in depth, or would scanning many subjects make a better presentation? Many potential authors never get beyond this stage of questioning. I wanted to go further. I had to give myself a framework and a challenge.

Here is what I came up with. I played an "old tape" I heard many years ago, an old tape that kept on repeating that Canadians and Americans are the same. This book will attempt to erase parts of that old tape and insert updated segments that accurately compare Canadians and Americans as we now live our lives.

The old tape is based on the concept that Canadians, when taken as a whole, are merely one-tenth of what Americans are and, therefore, there is no need to compare them. The old tape can be summarized as the "rule of 10:1". The concept behind the old tape angers me because I know it is both incorrect and disrespectful to Canadians and Canada. I first encountered the concept in the 1960s and early 1970s, and it is still expressed today. Many Europeans and Americans, and even some Canadians, believe that we are merely a mini-U.S.A.

I accept that we are indeed similar to Americans in many ways, and this book substantiates that reality. But it also reveals that Canadians are profoundly different from Americans in many important ways—in ways we think and in things we do. Some of the differences are favourable; some are unfavourable.

This short chapter confirms that Canadian output, employment and population are indeed about one-tenth of American output, employment and population. Is the old tape still playing? No! Further analysis will reveal that the rule of 10:1 does not work all that often. Canadians and Americans do things in different ratios, and come from different places. Canadians talk about languages and Americans talk about race. Our ethnic origins and ancestries are different. Our health-care systems are different. Our social systems vary widely. And sometimes we talk different, eh?

The following chapters provide additional material for revising the old tape. By the end of the book a "new tape" will portray a more accurate description of Canadians and Americans.

1 / THE RULE OF 10:1 IS NOT GOOD ENOUGH

Some people say it is very easy to compare our two countries. Just use the "rule of 10:1" which implies that Canada is equal to 1/10th of the United States.

Here is how it is supposed to work. Simply take an American total for some activity and multiply by .10 to get the Canadian total. Or, take a Canadian total for some indicator and multiply by 10 to get the American total.

This method works once in a while! Yes, Canada's total output is .097 (close to .10) of the output in the United States or, conversely, the United States produces 10.3 times what Canada produces. It also works fairly well for total employment and total population.

In contrast, there are many indicators that show we really are different. An extreme and stereotypical example: murder. The number of murders in the United States is 32 times that of Canada. This book takes you beyond the "rule of 10:1".

EXAMPLES OF THE RULE OF 10:1

	CANADA AS SHARE OF UNITED STATES	UNITED STATES AS A MULTIPLE OF CANADA
Situations When the "Rule of 10:1" Works Fairly Well		
Total output ('92):	.097	10.3
Total employment ('93):	.104	9.6
Total population ('91):	.108	9.2
Situations When the "Rule of 10:1" Does Not Work at All		
Self-employed women ('93):	.179	5.6
Unemployed ('93):	.179	5.6
Marriages ('91):	.073	13.8
Divorces ('91):	.065	15.4
Murders ('92):	.031	32.0

Sources: Statistics Canada, Catalogue 93-310, 71-220, 84-205, 85-002. U.S. Bureau of the Census, Statistical Abstracts of the United States; Bureau of Labor Statistics, Employment and Earnings. Organization for Economic Co-operation and Development (OECD) Economic Outlook.

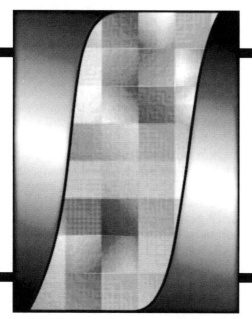

THE BIG PICTURE ABOUT PEOPLE AND PLACES

CANADIANS ARE FEW
AND AMERICANS
ARE MANY

This chapter lays out a few of the basic things readers should know about Canada and the United States.

The long economic and cultural shadow cast by the U.S. naturally forces us Canadians to compare ourselves to Americans. Canadians have an additional dilemma when we try to measure ourselves relative to Americans— should we use yardsticks or metres? Many Canadians are still not comfortable with the metric system, which has been in use for about two decades. I am still converting *this many centimetres* of snow into *that many inches* of snow, and Americans may be doing the same in the future.

Both Canada and the United States are relatively large countries in terms of land mass. Growing up in the second-largest country in the world gave me a good feeling, even a superior feeling. The U.S. ranks fourth.

For many years, Canada has been able to transform its natural wealth into income and security for Canadian people. Over the last decade this natural resource advantage seems to have been eroded somewhat by weak commodity prices and by a world which now competes more on ideas, innovation, and communication technology. In addition, worldwide environmental degradation is making me and other Canadians feel a bit guilty about using up our non-renewable resources.

In terms of population, Canada is relatively small while the United States is relatively large. Canadians are few and Americans are many.

It is not easy for me to accept the fact that California now has a larger population than all of Canada, or that metropolitan areas of New York and Los Angeles—take your pick—are more populated than all of the metropolitan areas in Canada combined.

I sometimes feel angry that Americans know little about Canada, but at the same time I have to admit that I am only familiar with about half of the 10 smallest American metropolitan areas. How many Canadians—or even Americans—can find Fort Pierce, U.S.A. on a map? Whatever the percentage of Canadians might be who can find Fort Pierce, I believe that more than 16 per cent of Americans should be able to find Canada's national capital on a map.

2/ COUNTING THE WARM BODIES

How many of us are out there? Canadians numbered 27,297,000 on June 4, 1991, when the last official census was taken. At the same time, Americans residing in the United States were estimated at 252,177,000. The actual number is somewhat higher in both countries due to undercounting.

Over the 15 years ending in 1991, Canada's population grew by 17 per cent, or just a bit more than the 16 per cent advance for the United States. From that point to the middle of the next decade, the population of Canada is projected to increase about 19 per cent to 33 million, while the population of the United States is forecast to grow by 16 per cent to 289 million. Higher immigration to Canada explains much of the difference.

Canada is a relatively small country in terms of population—it ranks 32nd behind Argentina's 33 million. In contrast, the United States ranks third in the world behind China's 1.1 billion and India's 900 million.

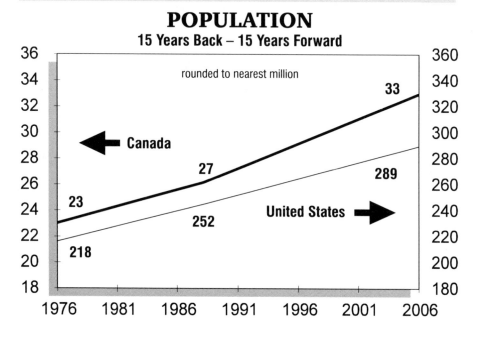

POPULATION
15 Years Back – 15 Years Forward

Sources: Statistics Canada, special tabulation for author. Statistics Canada, Catalogue 93-310. U.S. Bureau of the Census, Statistical Abstracts of the United States and Current Population Report P25-1092.

3/DIFFERENT ROOTS

The way we are classified by the official data collectors reveals much about the way we have looked at ourselves in the past—and still do.

Ongoing debate suggests that language is one of the important ways to help define Canadians. Eighty-three per cent of Canadians speak English, 32 per cent speak French, and 16 per cent speak both of the two "officially" recognized languages. Almost one in five Canadians speaks other languages.

American statisticians tend to emphasize race. "Whites" comprise 84 per cent of the American population, with "Blacks" representing 12 per cent. "Hispanic" refers to persons who personally identify themselves as Hispanic and they can be of any race. They make up 9 per cent of all Americans.

Canadians and Americans have divergent ethnic and ancestral origins. It is noteworthy that only 3 per cent of Canadians and 5 per cent of Americans say their ethnic origins are the country they now live in.

In terms of religion, Catholics are the largest group in Canada while Protestants make up the majority in the United States. Over 10 per cent declare they have no religious affiliation.

BACKGROUND CHARACTERISTICS

	CANADA 1991		UNITED STATES 1990	
Languages spoken:			*Race:*	
English	83%		White	84%
French	32%		Black	12%
English and French	16%		Other	4%
Non-official	19%		Hispanic*	9%
			(*can be any race)	
Ethnic origin:			*Ancestry:*	
French	23%		German	23%
English	21%		Irish	16%
Canadian	3%		English	13%
German	3%		Italian	6%
Italian	3%		American	5%
Chinese	2%		French	4%
Aboriginal	2%		Polish	4%
All other	43%		Amer-Indian, Eskimo, Aleut	1%

Religion:		*Religion:*	
Catholic	46%	Protestant	56%
Protestant	36%	Catholic	25%
Other	5%	Other	8%
No religion	13%	No religion	11%

Sources: Statistics Canada, Catalogue 93-317, 93-315, 93-319. U.S. Bureau of the Census, Statistical Abstracts of the United States.

4/COMPARING HOUSEHOLDS AND FAMILIES

A family is a household, but a household may not be a family. Confused? A simple definition may help. If you live in a house, then you automatically live in a household. If you live with someone with whom you are related, then you are considered to be part of a family.

In Canada, common-law couples without children are assumed to be related, and are therefore part of a family. This is not always the case in the United States. All other persons are listed as living in "non-family households" and are interchangeably labelled "unattached" or "unrelated" individuals, whether or not they live alone or with others.

In Canada, there are 22.6 million people living in 7.3 million families, which produces an average family size of 3.1 people. The average American family is just a bit larger: 3.2 persons.

Non-family households are bigger in Canada at 1.6 persons compared to 1.3 in the United States.

SUMMARY OF HOUSEHOLDS AND FAMILIES – 1991

	CANADA	UNITED STATES
	(millions)	
Population in private households:	26.7	248.0
- population in family households	22.6	210.9
- population in non-family households	4.2	37.1
Number of private households:	10.0	94.3
- number of family households	7.3	66.3
- number of non-family households	2.7	28.0
Average Household Sizes by Type		
Persons per private household:	2.7	2.6
- persons per family household	3.1	3.2
- persons per non-family household	1.6	1.3

Sources: Statistics Canada, Catalogue 93-311, 93-312. U.S. Bureau of the Census, Statistical Abstracts of the United States.

5/CENTRES OF POPULATION ARE MOVING WEST IN BOTH COUNTRIES

Canada's land mass of 10 million square km (3.9 million square miles) is the second largest in the world behind Russia. The United States, at 9.4 million square km (3.6 million square miles), is the fourth-largest country behind China.

One change is similar in both countries—the population is slowly shifting west. The centres are calculated somewhat differently in each country, but roughly represent that point in each country that could be reached with the least total travel distance.

Canada's centre of population is the small township of Laxton, Digby, and Longford in Ontario, about 62 km (38.5 miles) northeast of Toronto Census Metropolitan Area (CMA). Over the last 20 years, it has moved westward by about 50 km (31 miles). Canada's centre of population was near Montreal when Canada celebrated Confederation.

The U.S. centre of population is now about 15.6 km (9.7 miles) southeast of Steelville, in Missouri, east of St. Louis. The American centre crossed the Illinois/Missouri border during the 1970s. The United States centre of population was near Baltimore, Maryland when the United States declared independence in 1776.

CENTRES OF POPULATION

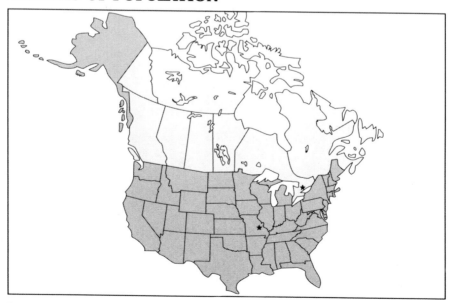

Sources: Statistics Canada, *All Roads Lead to Laxton, Digby and Longford,* Census of Canada. U.S. Bureau of the Census, Statistical Abstracts of the United States.

6/CALIFORNIA HAS A LARGER POPULATION THAN ALL OF CANADA

The entire population of Canada is less than the 30.4 million people who live in California. California moved ahead of Canada during the early 1980s.

A ranking of Canadian provinces and American states reveals that Ontario is the eighth most populated behind California, New York, Texas, Florida, Pennsylvania, Illinois and Ohio. Quebec ranks in 11th position.

The next most peopled province is British Columbia, in 30th spot. A few steps beyond are Alberta in 36th and Manitoba in 46th positions respectively.

The remaining provinces all have a population base of less than one million. Wyoming is the least populous state at 460,000; Prince Edward Island is the least populous province at 130,000 and it is also, in terms of area, the smallest province.

Canada's Yukon and Northwest Territories have a combined population of 81,000. Outlying areas of the United States include 3.5 million people in Puerto Rico, plus 325,000 more in American Samoa, Guam, the Virgin Islands and Northern Mariana Islands.

PROVINCES AND STATES RANKED BY POPULATION SIZE – 1991

	000's	Rank
California	30380	1
New York	18058	2
Texas	17349	3
Florida	13277	4
Pennsylvania	11961	5
Illinois	11543	6
Ohio	10939	7
ONTARIO	10085	8
Michigan	9368	9
New Jersey	7760	10
QUEBEC	6896	11
North Carolina	6737	12
Georgia	6623	13
Virginia	6286	14
Massachusetts	5996	15
Indiana	5610	16
Missouri	5158	17
Washington	5018	18
Wisconsin	4955	19

Tennessee	4953	20
Maryland	4860	21
Minnesota	4432	22
Louisiana	4252	23
Alabama	4089	24
Arizona	3750	25
Kentucky	3713	26
South Carolina	3560	27
Colorado	3377	28
Connecticut	3291	29
BRITISH COLUMBIA	3282	30
Oklahoma	3175	31
Oregon	2922	32
Iowa	2795	33
Mississippi	2592	34
Kansas	2495	35
ALBERTA	2546	36
Arkansas	2372	37
West Virginia	1801	38
Utah	1770	39
Nebraska	1593	40
New Mexico	1548	41
Nevada	1284	42
Maine	1235	43
Hawaii	1135	44
New Hampshire	1105	45
MANITOBA	1092	46
Idaho	1039	47
Rhode Island	1004	48
SASKATCHEWAN	989	49
NOVA SCOTIA	900	50
Montana	808	51
NEW BRUNSWICK	724	52
South Dakota	703	53
Delaware	680	54
North Dakota	635	55
Alaska	570	56
NEWFOUNDLAND	569	57
Vermont	567	58
Wyoming	460	59
PRINCE EDWARD ISLAND	130	60

Sources: Statistics Canada, Catalogue 93-310. U.S. Bureau of the Census, Statistical Abstracts of the United States.

7/MAJORITY LIVE IN METROPOLITAN AREAS

Most of us live in metropolitan areas. U.S. statisticians define these as "very large urban areas, together with adjacent areas which have a high degree of economic and social integration."

At present, 61 per cent of Canadians and 78 per cent of Americans live in metropolitan centres. In Canada, the term "urban area" includes any locality with 1,000 or more people. Using the Canadian definition, about eight out of 10 Canadians and Americans now live in urban areas.

Metropolitan areas provide most of the population advances. During the last decade, virtually all (98 per cent) of the growth in Canada and 90 per cent of the growth in the United States took place in metropolitan areas. Some of this growth was due to changes in boundary definitions.

The largest metropolitan centre is New York City with over 19 million people, followed by Los Angeles with almost 15 million. Toronto's 4 million ranks just ahead of Dallas. Saint John and Charleston are the smallest metropolitan areas in Canada and the United States respectively.

METROPOLITAN AREAS
(000's of persons/census in early 1990s)

CANADA		UNITED STATES	
		10 Largest Metropolitan Areas	
Toronto	4040	New York	19342
Montreal	3215	Los Angeles	14532
Vancouver	1949	Chicago	8242
Ottawa	953	Washington/Baltimore	6727
Edmonton	857	San Francisco	6253
Calgary	769	Philadelphia	5893
Winnipeg	665	Boston	5455
Quebec	663	Detroit	5187
Hamilton	621	Dallas	4037
London	398	Houston	3731

CANADA   UNITED STATES
10 Smallest Metropolitan Areas

Canada		United States	
Windsor	272	Erie	276
Oshawa	249	Fayetteville	275
Saskatoon	214	Binghampton	264
Regina	195	Provo	264
St. John's	175	Springfield	264
Chicoutimi	165	Columbus	261
Sudbury	163	Savannah	258
Sherbrooke	143	Reno	255
Trois-Rivières	140	Fort Pierce	251
Saint John	130	Charleston	250

Sources: Statistics Canada, Catalogue 93-310. U.S. Bureau of the Census, Statistical Abstracts of the United States.

8/ NOT ALL PLACES ARE THE SAME

What is good and bad about the place where you live?

In *Places Rated Almanac,* David Savageau and Richard Boyer have developed a system to rank all of the 343 Census Metropolitan Areas (CMAs) in Canada and the United States. Their rankings are based on 10 criteria: living costs, job outlook, housing, transportation, education, health care, crime, the arts, recreation and climate.

Their ranking system places Cincinnati, Seattle and Philadelphia as the top three places to live, with Toronto ranking fourth. Pittsburgh and Raleigh round out the top five in the United States. Vancouver ranks 11th overall.

The 36 worst places to live are all in the United States—Yuba City is number 343. The authors rank Chicoutimi 307th and as the worse place to live in Canada. Canadian CMAs are generally pulled down by climate because a mean of 65 degrees Fahrenheit is considered ideal.

PLACES RATED ALMANAC'S BEST AND WORST PLACES TO LIVE

The Five Best in Each Country and Their Best Feature

CANADA		UNITED STATES	
Toronto	Arts	Cincinnati	Jobs
Vancouver	Climate	Seattle	Recreation
Quebec City	Little Crime	Philadelphia	Health
Montreal	Health	Pittsburgh	Education
Halifax	Health	Raleigh	Jobs

The Five Worst in Each Country and Their Worst Feature

Trois-Rivières	Transportation	Albany	Transportation
Saint John	Education	Sumter	Health Care
Thunder Bay	Climate	Waterbury	Recreation
Sudbury	Climate	Merced	Recreation
Chicoutimi	Climate	Yuba City	Education

Source: David Savageau and Richard Boyer, *Places Rated Almanac.* Toronto: Prentice Hall, 1993.

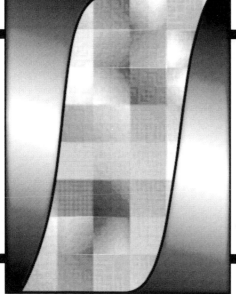

HOW CANADIANS AND AMERICANS LOOK AT EACH OTHER

HERE'S LOOKING AT YOU...FRIEND? SNOB?

What do Canadians think of Americans, and what do Americans think of Canadians? Are we close in our thinking? Are we friends? Do we really care about each other? What kind of relationship do we want in the future? These are questions that individual Canadians ask frequently, but they are questions that Americans seem to care much less about.

Like it or not, Canadians and Americans are stuck in a relationship. Many Canadians feel that our American partners don't care about anyone but themselves. This may stem from a feeling of neglect and non-recognition by Americans. Americans seem to take Canada for granted, and many Canadians don't like it.

Canadians know that we must continue to have a relationship with Americans—we just aren't overly happy about the longstanding one-sided nature of that relationship. This may explain why many Canadians think Americans project a superior attitude and frequently think of them as snobs. In contrast, Americans think Canadians are "friendly" and "nice," and there seems to be "nothing" that Americans don't like about Canadians. The word "nothing" reveals an ignorance about real Canadians and Canada. Would Americans still think we are friendly if they knew us better?

Many Canadians feel that Americans have an ulterior motive: Americans would like Canada to become the 51st American state, or at least have first pick on accessing our water and other natural resources. Canadians, on the other hand, don't want to join the United States. Canadians may argue amongst themselves but have no intention of becoming Americans.

Even so, the vast majority of Americans and a slim majority of Canadians think we are indeed more similar than we are different. Canadians place great value on the differences. This is so because we either are different, or desperately want to be different. We are not Americans, eh!

Notwithstanding all of the above, Canadians continue to like Americans, but do we think of them as our best friends?

9/AMERICANS' WARMTH FOR CANADIANS IS NOT RECIPROCATED

I like you, but do you feel the same way? A *Maclean's*/Decima survey answers part of the question.

Canadians and Americans yield very similar ratings relative to the attractiveness of the men and women of the other country. It is good to know that the ratings of 6.2 and 6.3 are both on the attractive (and not the ugly) side of the scale.

Canadians and Americans were asked to describe each other using only one word. The three most popular words used by Canadians to describe Americans were "snobs," followed by "good" and then "friendly." In contrast, Americans chose "friendly" as the best single word to describe Canadians—this word won by a longshot—with "nice" and "neighbours" far behind.

The trait that Canadians like least about Americans is their "superior attitude." Meanwhile, the largest group of Americans could not think of anything they did not like about Canadians, or said that they did not know Canadians.

HOW WE RATE EACH OTHER – 1989

	Canadians towards Americans	Americans towards Canadians
Attractiveness of men/women in the other country?		
-On a scale of 1 to 10:	6.2	6.3
Best word to describe people the in other country?		
-Most popular word:	Snobs 11%	Friendly 28%
-2nd most popular word:	Good 9%	Nice 9%
-3rd most popular word:	Friendly 8%	Neighbours 6%
What you like least about people in other country?		
-Most mentioned trait:	Superior attitude/ 25%	Nothing 37%

Source: Maclean's, "Portrait of Two Nations." July 3, 1989.

10/CANADIANS SAY "NO" TO JOINING THE UNITED STATES

Do you think Canada and the United States should become one?

According to a *Maclean's*/Decima survey conducted on both sides of the border, only 14 per cent of Canadians favour becoming the 51st American state while two-thirds of Americans like the idea.

Only 27 per cent of Canadians say they would like to live in the United States; 42 per cent of Americans say they would like to live in Canada. The reality indicates that the opposite prevails: there are more Canadians who actually emigrate south than there are Americans who move north.

A minority of Canadians would send their children to a university or college in the United States, while a majority of Americans would send their children to Canada.

The vast majority of Canadians want their own foreign policy while the majority of Americans would like to have a common policy. Almost half of Canadians would welcome a common currency with the United States—three-quarters of Americans like the idea.

POSSIBLE RELATIONS WITH NEIGHBOUR – 1989

	Canadians	Americans
On Canada becoming the 51st state -Favour/strongly favour:	14%	66%
Would like to live in the other country? -Yes:	27%	42%
Would like to send children to university/college in other country? -Yes:	41%	58%
Common policy on defence and foreign affairs? -Support/strongly support:	38%	73%
Adopt a common currency? -Favour/strongly favour:	49%	74%

Source: Maclean's, "Portrait of Two Nations." July 3, 1989.

11 /AMERICANS KNOW VERY LITTLE ABOUT CANADA

Canadians often claim that Americans know very little about Canada. Americans are guilty as charged!

A 1992 Gallup survey revealed that 93 per cent of Canadians could correctly name George Bush as the president of the United States. In contrast, only 13 per cent of Americans could name Brian Mulroney as the prime minister of Canada even though he had occupied that office for six and one-half years. Similar percentages from each group could correctly name Washington and Ottawa as the capital cities. Almost identical results were obtained in a 1989 survey.

The volume of two-way merchandise trade between Canada and the United States is 25 per cent greater than the two-way trade between Japan and the United States. Only 12 per cent of Americans know that Canada is indeed the United States' biggest trading partner. In contrast, 83 per cent of Canadians know that the United States is Canada's biggest trading partner.

Almost eight in 10 Canadians were aware of the 1992 proposals dealing with the North American Free Trade Agreement; only half of Americans were aware of the NAFTA proposals.

KNOWLEDGE OF OTHER COUNTRY – 1992

	Canadians	Americans
Could correctly identify the other country's prime minister/president:	93%	13%
Could correctly identify the other country's capital city:	90%	16%
Are aware that Canada and the United States are each other's biggest trading partner:	83%	12%
Awareness of NAFTA proposal:	79%	52%

Source: Gallup Canada, *The Gallup Report.*

12/AMERICANS ARE MORE LIKELY TO SEE SIMILARITIES

Do you think that Canadians and Americans are mostly different or mostly the same? *Maclean's*/Decima Research did the asking.

Perceived similarities win out in both countries, but especially among Americans. A small majority of Canadians (56 per cent) and a large majority of Americans (78 per cent) believe that we are "essentially" or "mainly" the same.

In contrast, 19 per cent of Canadians believe that we are essentially different compared to only 6 per cent of Americans who feel this way.

The finding that many more Americans think we are similar may reflect Americans' generally weaker knowledge base for making comparisons about "things Canadian." Part of the explanation is that Canadians are more exposed to the U.S. through American media than is the case in reverse, and that Canadians are generally more aware of the international scene. Of course, one of the reasons why many Canadians and Americans think we are similar is because, in many ways, we are.

HOW CANADIANS AND AMERICANS VIEW EACH OTHER – 1989

	Canadians	Americans
Essentially the same:	13%	18%
Mainly the same:	43%	60%
Mainly different:	24%	15%
Essentially different:	19%	6%

Source: Maclean's, "Portrait of Two Nations." July 3, 1989.

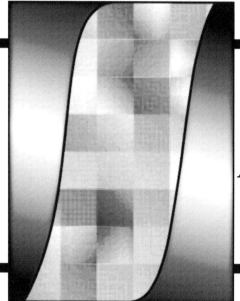

HOW CANADIANS AND AMERICANS LOOK AT THEMSELVES

THE SOULS OF TWO NEIGHBOURS

This chapter examines what Canadians and Americans think about a wide range of topics including such biggies as country, religion, sex and family. The key question is, "Do we look at the world around us through the same set of glasses?" Sometimes we do, and sometimes we don't.

Canadians are very proud of our country. Even so, our pride seems like a watered-down version of the almost fanatical pride expressed by Americans. Canadians are not flag wavers. I think this reflects our more reserved national character, the large number of Quebecers who are not proud of Canada at all, and the convergence of some negative attitudes that are receiving national expression. Canadians definitely show more dissatisfaction about the direction their country is going, and few can argue that taxes are not too high.

I see a paradox in the United States, however. Americans are so very proud, yet they don't they come out to vote. They don't like their health-care system. They have little confidence in most of their institutions. Americans are so very proud, but they harbour one of the highest poverty rates in the industrial world. And what about all the murders? How is it that Americans can be so proud with all the bad things that are part of their environment?

One thing that both Canadians and Americans have in common is their disappointment with their governments.

Americans seem to be hung up on the punitive aspects of religion. Almost double the percentage of Americans believe in the "devil" and "hell" than do Canadians. This preoccupation with the extremes of good and evil makes it difficult for Americans to practise the art of compromise and cooperation.

Canadians responses show more acceptance of alternative ways of thinking and behaving. This is true relative to euthanasia, gays in the military, premarital sex and sexual freedom in general.

Canada seems to be a more comfortable place to live. Maybe Canadians are friendlier and nicer after all!

13/ATTITUDES ARE MORE ALIKE THAN DIFFERENT

Do you think that Canadians and Americans have similar attitudes to social trends? Let's check it out.

In the United States, the *Yankelovich Monitor* has conducted a large-scale lifestyle tracking survey since 1971. Creative Research International Inc., a Canadian company, has adapted the *Yankelovich Monitor* to Canada. Their 1992 surveys questioned Canadians and Americans about their feelings relative to 41 social trends in their respective countries.

The results indicate that Canadians and Americans show large differences in attitudes for only 10 per cent of the social trends examined, plus "significant but moderate differences" for another 15 per cent of the trends—a cumulative 25 per cent difference. A 1990 survey found differences for 28 per cent of the social trends.

No statistically "significant" responses were found for 75 per cent of the trends. The 1990 survey found 72 per cent of the trends were viewed similarly. These findings support the view that Canadians and Americans exhibit many *similar* attitudes but differ enough in an appreciable number (25 per cent) of areas.

HOW CANADIANS AND AMERICANS COMPARE RELATIVE TO 41 SOCIAL ATTITUDES – 1992

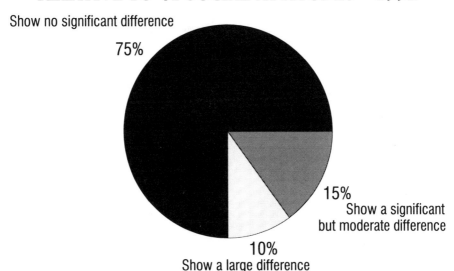

Show no significant difference
75%

15%
Show a significant
but moderate difference

10%
Show a large difference

Source: Creative Research International Inc.

14/CANADIANS ARE NOT AS PROUD OF COUNTRY

How proud are you to be a Canadian or an American? Let us count the ways!

Polls conducted by Gallup in 1991 found that 89 per cent of Canadians were very or quite proud to be Canadian compared to 96 per cent among Americans relative to their country. Very high rates for both countries! The end of the Persian Gulf war likely added a few more points to American patriotism than it did in Canada. At the same time, Americans are more likely to say they spend too much on defence.

Canadians show their pride and commitment by consistently coming out to vote in much larger numbers.

Fewer Canadians say they are content to stay in their own country; in 1992, more were dissatisfied with the direction the country was going and Canadians were less optimistic regarding the future. Canadians pay more taxes and they also complain more about them—the 22 percentage point spread with respect to the level of taxation is the largest of any measure on this page.

Canadians are much more likely to say they have an excellent or good health system.

PRIDE AND SATISFACTION WITH COUNTRY

	Canadians		**Americans**	
Very/quite proud to be Canadian/American:	89%	('91)	96%	('91)
Voter turnout/national elections:	73%	('80s)	54%	('80s)
Content to stay in own country:	76%	('91)	90%	('91)
Dissatisfied with direction country is going:	76%	('92)	68%	('93)
Excellent or good health care:	71%	('92)	59%	('92)
See rising standard of living in future/next generation:	23%	('93)	28%	('92)
Taxes too high (agree):	77%	('93)	55%	('93)
Too much spending on defence (agree):	33%	('91)	42%	('93)

Sources: Gallup Canada, *The Gallup Report. The Gallup Poll Monthly* (U.S.). Statistics Canada, *Canadian Social Trends,* Winter 1992.

15/ NOT MANY INSTITUTIONS LEFT TO HANG ON TO

We have created institutions to help us achieve our goals and aspirations. Both Canadians and Americans are losing confidence in these institutions.

Over the last decade, Gallup surveys have recorded declines or, at best, flat levels of respect and confidence in the institutions on both sides of the border.

Canadians bestow their highest level of respect on the Supreme Court, but even here only half of Canadians have a "great deal" or "quite a lot" of respect and confidence in this institution. Just over half of Americans have a great or quite a bit of respect and confidence in church and organized religion.

These are the only institutions hitting the 50 per cent mark. Canadians have more respect for the public school system.

Respect is similar (and low) in both countries relative to newspapers, large corporations and big business, legislative élites and labour unions. Ratings of unions have changed very little in the last decade.

RESPECT AND CONFIDENCE IN INSTITUTIONS – 1993

	Canadians	Americans
Have a great deal/quite a lot of respect and confidence in:		
Supreme Court:	50%	43%
Public schools:	44%	39%
Church, organized religion:	41%	53%
Newspapers:	27%	31%
Large corporations/Big business:	22%	23%
Labour unions:	19%	26%
House of Commons/Congress:	16%	19%

Sources: Gallup Canada, *The Gallup Report. The Gallup Poll Monthly* (U.S.).

16/DEVIL HAS A BIGGER FOLLOWING IN AMERICA

Don't tell an American to "go to hell" because he or she may actually worry about it.

Over 70 per cent of Canadians and almost 80 per cent of Americans believe in "heaven." Attendance at a church, synagogue or other place of worship is lower in Canada, and attendance has been relatively stable in both countries over the last decade. About one-quarter of Canadians and Americans believe in reincarnation.

The punitive aspects of religion are much stronger in the United States where 60 per cent of Americans believe in "hell" and over half believe in the "devil." Only about a third of Canadians believe in these punitive concepts. Witches don't fare too well in either country.

Attitudes towards abortion are similar. About one-third in both countries support abortion under all circumstances, and about one-half approve of the abortion pill. A large (and growing) majority favour euthanasia in both countries.

ATTITUDES ON RELIGION AND SPIRITUALITY

	Canadians	Americans
Attended church, synagogue or other place of worship during last seven days:	35% ('93)	41% ('91)
Believe in heaven:	71% ('90)	78% ('91)
Believe in reincarnation:	26% ('90)	23% ('91)
Believe in hell:	34% ('90)	60% ('91)
Believe in the devil:	30% ('90)	52% ('91)
Believe in witches:	18% ('92)	16% ('91)
Abortion should be legal under all circumstances:	31% ('93)	32% ('93)
Approve of abortion pill:	48% ('92)	54% ('93)
Legalize euthanasia:	77% ('92)	65% ('91)

Sources: Gallup Canada, *The Gallup Report. The Gallup Poll Monthly* (U.S.).

17/SEXUAL FREEDOM MORE ACCEPTED BY CANADIANS

Gender issues encompass a wide range of topics that go far beyond the "battle of the sexes."

The search for equality is being fought on many fronts. Women still have a long way to go. Gallup surveys indicate that only 40 per cent in both countries believe that women get as good a deal as men at home or in the workplace. This belief has not changed during the last decade.

Two-thirds of Canadians now believe that gays should be allowed in the military compared to just under 60 per cent in the United States. Acceptance has been rising in both countries.

More Canadians say they welcome more sexual freedom and more are claiming that premarital sex is not wrong. In contrast, the vast majority of both Canadians and Americans believe extramarital affairs are wrong.

Romance is not dead. The majority of Canadians and Americans give cards on Valentine's Day, but Americans are more likely than Canadians to spend money on flowers and candies.

SEXUAL AND GENDER ATTITUDES

	Canadians		Americans	
Believe women get as good a deal as men:	41%	('93)	42%	('90)
Allow gays into military:	67%	('92)	57%	('92)
Welcome more acceptance of sexual freedom:	40%	('93)	29%	('91)
Premarital sex is not wrong:	70%	('92)	54%	('91)
Extramarital sex is wrong:	81%	('92)	91%	('91)
Valentine's Day intentions:				
-to give valentine	66%	('91)	56%	('92)
-to give flowers	30%	('91)	45%	('92)
-to give chocolates/candies	20%	('91)	27%	('92)

Sources: Gallup Canada, *The Gallup Report. The Gallup Poll Monthly* (U.S.).

18/LITTLE DIFFERENCE REGARDING FAMILY VALUES

Families are important to both Canadians and Americans, and both want to bring back or keep some of the more traditional values.

About 60 per cent of Gallup survey respondents say the ideal number of children is two or fewer. Big families are out.

Very similar percentages of Canadians and Americans would welcome more emphasis on traditional family values and less emphasis on money. Working hard is an accepted trait in both countries. About 12 per cent would welcome more acceptance of marijuana use.

The battle of the bulge has hit both sides of the border with exactly 35 per cent describing themselves as overweight. The percentage who smoke is also the same in both countries. Canadians are more likely to use alcohol.

Canadians feel safer on the streets, but are still more likely to push for more restrictive gun control laws.

FAMILY AND INDIVIDUAL ATTITUDES

	Canadians		Americans	
Ideal number of children is two or fewer:	59%	('91)	60%	('90)
Would welcome:				
-more emphasis on traditional family values	87%	('93)	94%	('91)
-less emphasis on money	68%	('93)	69%	('91)
-less emphasis on working hard	28%	('93)	29%	('91)
-more acceptance of marijuana use	14%	('93)	12%	('91)
Describe self as overweight:	35%	('92)	35%	('91)
Smoked during previous week:	29%	('93)	28%	('91)
Use alcohol:	76%	('92)	64%	('92)
Fear about walking in neighbourhood alone at night:	35%	('93)	44%	('92)
Favour more restrictive gun control laws:	77%	('94)	70%	('93)

Sources: Gallup Canada, *The Gallup Report. The Gallup Poll Monthly* (U.S.).

19/FOUR SETS OF TWINS?

Are there cities in the other country that make you think of home?

PRIZM Canada, a joint venture of Canadian-based Compusearch and American-based Claritas/NPDC, developed a system of neighbourhood clusters wherein the people who live inside each cluster have similar social and demographic characteristics. The system uncovered four "statistically" matched twins.

Ottawa-Hull and Washington, D.C. are one of these pairs. Both are national capitals, and both have strong white-collar, low-risk, conservative demographic structures. Their similarities are stronger than their differences, although crime rates are much higher in Washington.

Calgary and Denver are another set—both dependent on oil and tourism—and characterized by upscale white-collar workers with few ethnic or poor neighbourhoods.

The pairing of Saskatoon and Tuscon is based on high concentrations of young renters who are subject to unemployment, plus high shares of retirees from high-paying jobs. The other twin match is Hamilton and Detroit; both are aging industrial centres.

TWIN CITIES

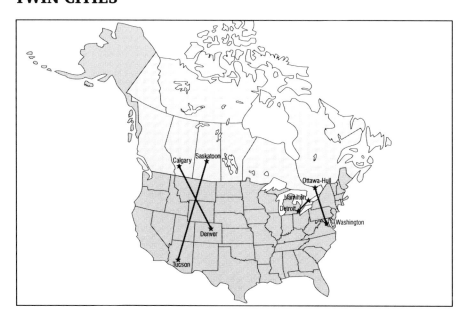

Source: American Demographics, June 1993.

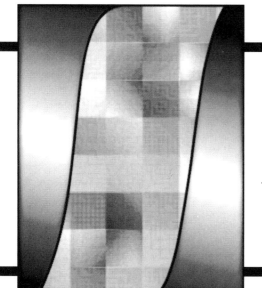

*LIFE
PATTERNS*

LONGER LIVE CANADIANS

Let's examine some of the elements affecting population growth in Canada and the United States.

No doubt about it—I would rather be born in Canada. First of all, I am more likely to survive the birth itself. Second, I am more likely to have a healthy birth weight. Most important, I will live longer in Canada. I believe that most of these factors are due to Canada's much superior health insurance system—and it costs much less than the American system. More suffering among poor Americans reflects the weakness of the American health and income system.

Life expectancy among Canadians has also been improving much faster than is the case for Americans. The Canadian health care system makes me very proud. (Can Americans do as well or better when they figure out what they want? I hope so, but I don't think so.)

The typical American woman is currently bringing just a fraction more babies into the world than are Canadian women. Bigger differences in childbearing relate to the age of the childbearers. American women are having their babies at a younger age—the birth rate for American teenagers is twice what it is among Canadian teenagers. Births to women in their 30s have soared in the 1980s in both countries, as have births to unwed mothers. The social fabric of families is changing much faster than the pace of public debate and policy decisions on family issues.

Take a look at immigration numbers. Canada is accepting international immigrants at rates two to three times higher than the United States. The pace of Canadian immigration has swung sharply upwards since the mid-1980s. I value the positive long-term benefits of immigration, but I feel that the pace of immigration should also reflect the short-term unemployment conditions in Canada. In the long term, Canada needs even more immigration. However, it needs less during recessionary and early recovery periods such as those experienced in recent years. In my view, immigration during recessions should be limited to filling specific labour shortages, adoptions and immediate family reunification, and in response to international disasters.

20/CANADIANS EXTEND LIFE EXPECTANCY OVER AMERICANS

You can expect to live longer if you live in Canada, especially if you are female.

Today, baby girls born in Canada can expect to live to about 81 years. Ten years have been added to Canadian females' life expectancies since the early 1950s, and only 7.5 years for American females.

Canadian and American males can expect to live to age 74 and 72 respectively. Canadian males have added almost eight years since the early 1950s compared to a 6.5 year life extension for American men.

Much of the Canadian advantage is due to a lower mortality rate among young babies and children. Differences tend to disappear as people age—a 40-year-old Canadian woman can expect to live eight months longer than her American counterpart; for Canadian men the advantage is reduced to only five months. Gallup surveys in the United States suggest that the average person would like to live to about 85 years.

LIFE EXPECTANCY AT BIRTH

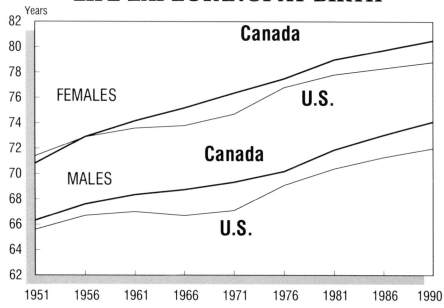

Sources: Statistics Canada, Catalogue 91-209. U.S. Bureau of the Census, Statistical Abstracts of the United States. *The Gallup Poll Monthly* (U.S.).

21 /AMERICAN WOMEN ARE NOW HAVING MORE BABIES

Demographers claim that a society needs a minimum number of babies in order to merely replace itself. The required natural replacement level is assumed to be 2.1 babies per adult woman: one male offspring, one female offspring, and an allowance for infertility and premature deaths.

The actual level of fertility (children during lifetime) impacts population levels in the short term and even more over the long term as offspring form the basis of support and dependency in the future.

During the Baby Boom (roughly 1946 to 1964), the Canadian fertility rate always exceeded the American rate with the difference gradually narrowing by the end of that period. At its peak (1959), the Canadian fertility rate hit over 3.9 children per woman, while in the United States the peak was 3.8 (1957). Fertility rates fell below the replacement rate at exactly the same time, in 1972. The rates rose again during the second half of the 1980s. The American rate is now just under 2.1, and in Canada it is near 1.8.

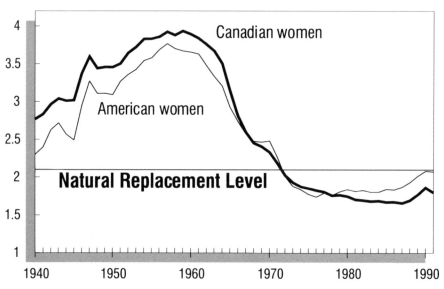

TOTAL FERTILITY RATE
CHILDREN PER WOMAN DURING LIFETIME

Sources: Statistics Canada, Catalogue 82-553. U.S. Bureau of the Census, Statistical Abstracts of the United States.

22/THE "MURPHY BROWN" BABY BOOM

The 1980s produced a small increase in the average number of children that women are having over a lifetime.

The increase in births in both Canada and the United States was a virtual boom among women 30 years old and up. Canadian and American women aged 30 to 34 both had birth rate advances of more than 25 per cent over the last decade. Women aged 35 to 39 experienced an even bigger jump of more than 50 per cent.

Rates for women 25 to 29 were flat in Canada and rose only 6 per cent in the United States. The rate for women under age 25 fell in Canada while it rose in the United States. All rates remain much lower than during the Baby Boom.

Compared to American women, Canadian women have, as a general rule, much lower fertility rates from ages 15 to 24, higher rates from 25 to 34, and a bit lower thereafter.

BIRTH RATE BY AGE OF MOTHER
(children born per 1,000 women in each age group)

Age of Mother	Canadians 1980/1991		Americans 1980/1991	
15-19	28	27	53	62
20-24	100	83	115	116
25-29	129	128	112	118
30-34	69	88	62	80
35-39	19	29	20	32

Sources: Statistics Canada, Catalogue 82-553. U.S. Bureau of the Census, Statistical Abstracts of the United States.

23/YOUNGER MOTHERS AND MORE ABORTIONS AMONG AMERICANS

The average number of children born over a mother's lifetime is now a bit lower for Canadians than Americans. Bigger differences appear elsewhere.

American women are more likely to have babies while single. About 30 per cent of American babies are born to an unwed mother compared to 25 per cent for Canadians. The American ratio is under 20 per cent for "white" women, and over 60 per cent for "black" women. The highest rate by group in Canada is for "aboriginals," at about 50 per cent.

The share of all births to teenagers is twice as high for Americans as for Canadians.

Americans are more likely to have babies born underweight. The infant mortality rate is also higher for Americans: the rate for "black" babies is 17 per 1,000 live births compared to eight for "white" babies.

One key difference between countries relates to the rate of abortion. In the United States there are about 400 abortions for every 1,000 live births to women aged 15 to 44—more than double the Canadian rate.

SELECTED BIRTH STATISTICS

Canadians	Americans
TOTAL FERTILITY RATE	
(children per woman during lifetime)	
1.8 (1991)	2.1 (1991)
BIRTHS TO UNWED MOTHERS	
(births to unwed mothers as a percentage of all births)	
25% (1991)	30% (1991)
BIRTHS TO TEENAGERS	
(births to teenagers as a percentage of all births)	
6% (1991)	13% (1991)
LOW BIRTH WEIGHTS	
(percentage of births with weights of less than 2,500 grams)	
5.5% (1991)	7.0% (1991)
INFANT MORTALITY	
(deaths per 1,000 live births)	
6.8 (1990)	9.2 (1990)
ABORTIONS	
(abortions per 1,000 live births for women aged 15 to 44)	
175 (1991)	401 (1988)

Sources: Statistics Canada, Catalogue 82-553, 82-003. U.S. Bureau of the Census, Statistical Abstracts of the United States.

24/IMMIGRATION IS MORE SIGNIFICANT TO CANADA

Fertility, death rates and international immigration are the three sources of population change. Together, they set the pace of total population growth.

Over the last 40 years, the number of international immigrants as a percentage of the growth in population has been much higher and more volatile in Canada than in the United States. During the 1950s and 1960s, immigrants comprised 40 per cent of Canadian population growth, and the ratio rose to over 50 per cent during the last two decades.

In the United States, the contribution of immigration was less than 10 per cent during the 1950s and increased to over 25 per cent during portions of the last decade.

The Canadian trend has moved sharply upwards since the mid-1980s, while the U.S. rate has remained relatively flat.

At the time of the latest census, about 16 per cent the Canadian population was foreign-born compared to 8 per cent for the American population. The origin of immigration to Canada is increasingly from Asia, South America and Africa—in 1991, almost two-thirds of immigrants came from these areas as compared to one-quarter in 1971. These three areas represent about half of all immigrants to the United States during the 1980s, compared with over 20 per cent during the 1960s.

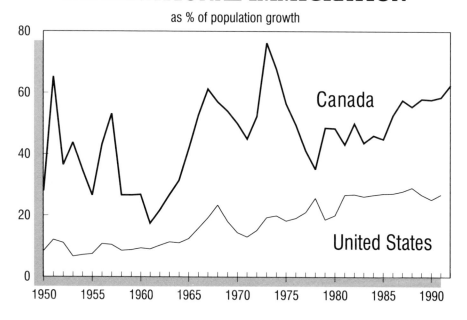

INTERNATIONAL IMMIGRATION
as % of population growth

Sources: Statistics Canada, Catalogue 11-210. U.S. Bureau of the Census, Statistical Abstracts of the United States.

25/MANY CANADIANS AND AMERICANS ARE "DOING THE SWITCH"

Canadians say they are less willing to move to the United States than is the case from the opposite direction. Actual migration data contradicts this perception.

Migration of Canadians to the United States has, on a fairly consistent basis, been greater than the reverse flow. The exception was from 1968 to 1976 and likely reflects the impact of the Vietnam war and major changes to Canadian and American immigration laws. The more recent flow of Canadians to the United States has been at least double the flow in the opposite direction.

A study done during the early 1980s examined the characteristics of these cross-border movers. Most Canadians who moved to the United States after 1960 live further south than earlier migrants. Americans who came to Canada after 1960 are more likely to live in Ontario and British Columbia. Migrants between the two countries have higher average incomes and education levels than the population who did not move. Roughly half of migrants have highly skilled occupations.

TWO-WAY MIGRATION

Source: U.S. Bureau of the Census, Current Population Report P23-161.

AGE
FUTURES

NO COASTING FOR BABY BOOMERS

Forecasting future levels of population is fun, it is fairly easy to do and, best of all, it provides many useful insights.

The key insight is one we already hear a lot about—baby boomers are aging. The boomers are now about 30 to 50 years old. The youngest are entering the last phases of having children, while the oldest boomers are ready to become empty-nesters...I'm there and I love it!

In both Canada and the United States, the number of working boomers will remain high for at least another 15 years before they begin to retire. This means that both countries have a long enough period of time to plan and adjust public pension and health systems. Contrary to popular belief, the number of dependants per person of working age will be lower in 15 years than it is today. But neither country can afford to wait for a crisis to develop before taking fiscally sound steps to ensure a healthy future.

Canada's population structure is aging faster than is the case in the United States, due in large part to the fact that Canada had a higher fertility rate immediately before and during all of the baby boom.

The changing age structure of persons of working age poses a new kind of problem. Over the 15-year forecast period, both countries will experience small declines in the number of workers aged 24 to 44, while the number of persons over the age of 45 will soar.

The older group will have to become much more aggressive than in the past in upgrading their skills to match the rapidly changing demands of the workplace. The over-45s will not be able to coast to retirement—they will need to compete against a better-educated workforce, a workforce who badly want their jobs. The latest Canadian recession saw the steepest growth in unemployment among the 45-and-over age group, not among the youth group.

The future is here! Believe it, and get ready! Young workers will have bright futures due to their relative scarcity.

26/POPULATION FORECASTING—LET'S MAKE ASSUMPTIONS

Population forecasting is based on making assumptions about the direction of a few important trends. Will these trends rise, fall or stay the same?

The Canadian population forecasts presented in this book derive from my own set of assumptions which were run through a Statistics Canada model. The United States forecasts are based on the U.S. Bureau of the Census "middle" projection, issued in November 1993.

The forecasts 1) assume a flat fertility rate in Canada and the United States (a higher or lower fertility assumption would soon impact the number of pre-school, primary and secondary school-aged children. No other age groups would be impacted over the forecast period); 2) assume immigration levels are in line with government targets and interpretation of current laws; 3) assume that past longevity trends will hold true and that people will live longer in both countries.

The process leads to 33 million Canadians and 289 Americans by the middle of the next decade.

ASSUMPTIONS UNDERLYING POPULATION FORECASTS

	Canada Latest / 2006		United States Latest / 2005	
Total fertility rate:	1.8 (1991)	1.8	2.1 (1991)	2.1
Immigration (000s):	249 (1992)	250	742 (1990)	880
Life expectancy:	77.3 (1990)	79.9	75.7 (1991)	77.6

Sources: Statistics Canada, special tabulation for the author. U.S. Bureau of the Census, Statistical Abstracts of the United States and Current Population Report P25-1092.

27/CANADIANS TO AGE FASTER THAN AMERICANS

One way to measure the age of a nation is to determine the "median age." A person is at the median age when half of the nation's people are younger and half are older.

The median age of Canadians and Americans increased steadily from the beginning of this century and peaked around 1950. At that time, the median age approached 30 in both Canada and the United States. The Baby Boom altered this long-term trend—the median age declined until the mid-to-late 1960s with the low for both countries at under 28 years. The population has been aging again since then.

The outlook sees a continuation of this aging with the median age for Canadians rising to 38.5 years, and for Americans to 36.5 by the middle of the next decade. The assumptions suggest that the difference between Canadians and Americans will widen from 0.3 years during the early 1990s to 2.0 years at the end of the forecast period.

MEDIAN AGE
(age at which half the people are younger and half are older)

Canadians		Americans	
1991	33.4	1990	33.1
1996	35.3	1995	34.0
2001	37.1	2000	35.5
2006	38.5	2005	36.5

Sources: Statistics Canada, special tabulation for the author. U.S. Bureau of the Census, Statistical Abstracts of the United States and Current Population Report P25-1092.

28/A FLOOD OF EMPTY NESTERS

A useful way to look at population change is to combine statistics to form large groups which reflect different stages of life, and then compare the change in each of these groups with the change in the total population. These "big group" forecasts and comparisons can be considered fairly accurate in making 10- to 15-year projections.

The current growth among households in the "potential" child-raising group (aged roughly 18 to 49) will fizzle by the year 2000 and, in total, this group will grow by less than 10 per cent to the middle of the next decade.

Aging "boomers" will cause a flood in the number of empty nesters (aged 50 to 64) which will expand by about 50 per cent or more in both countries. Empty nesters will expand at a rate more than three times the pace of the total population.

The overall aging of the population will naturally push more people into the seniors (65+) age group. The growth of the seniors group in Canada will be roughly double the rate of that in the United States.

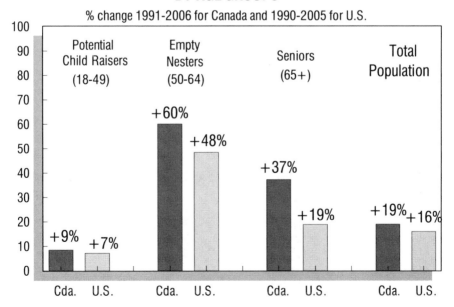

HOUSEHOLD POPULATIONS
BY AGE GROUPS
% change 1991-2006 for Canada and 1990-2005 for U.S.

Sources: Statistics Canada, special tabulation for the author. U.S. Bureau of the Census, Statistical Abstracts of the United States and Current Population Report P25-1092.

29/MORE PRIMARY SCHOOL STUDENTS AHEAD

Changes in fertility have near-term impacts on population predictions related to children, youth and school-aged populations.

The forecasts presented here see fertility remaining near current levels. This results in little change in the number of pre-schoolers in either country. This part of the 15-year forecast is the least certain—a continuation of the upward trend in fertility underway in the United States in the late 1980s would push the pre-school population up immediately.

The increase in fertility, especially during the late 1980s, has already set the pace for moderate growth in the number of primary and secondary school students. The more rapid rise in fertility for Americans during the 1980s is mirrored in a larger increase in population projected for this age group in the United States. A higher fertility rate in the near-term would cause this group to expand even more rapidly later in the forecast period.

University and post-secondary school populations will expand more quickly in Canada.

SCHOOL-AGE POPULATIONS
BY AGE GROUPS

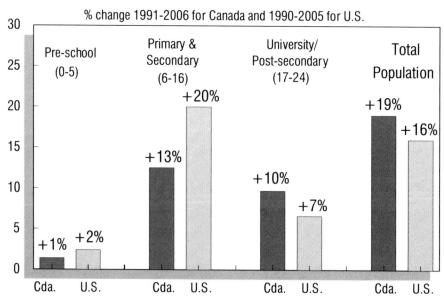

Sources: Statistics Canada, special tabulation for the author. U.S. Bureau of the Census, Statistical Abstracts of the United States and Current Population Report P25-1092.

30/AN OLDER GROUP OF WORKERS

A dramatic shift in age structures is evident among labour force or workforce age groups.

The majority of entry-level workers come from the under-25 age group. The size of this group actually shrank during the 1980s and is expected to display only moderate growth during the 15-year forecast period. This group will remain in relatively short supply and I believe will be in a favoured position in the job market.

Most "boomers" are already listed as maturing workers (ages 25 to 44) and they will remain the largest group in absolute terms as they gradually make the transition in a wave-like fashion into the older-worker category (ages 45 to 64). Their transition will continue into the middle of the next decade and beyond. The increases for older workers are forecast at 60 per cent in Canada and 52 per cent in the United States.

This wave will increase the demand for job retraining. Unemployed persons in this group may have a tougher time finding new employment.

WORKFORCE POPULATIONS
BY AGE GROUPS

Sources: Statistics Canada, special tabulation for the author. U.S. Bureau of the Census, Statistical Abstracts of the United States and Current Population Report P25-1092.

31 /DEPENDENCY RATIOS ARE DECLINING FOR NOW

Can we support ourselves in the future?

One way to assess the support system is to count the number of present and future "supporters" and "dependants" and see how the relationship between each is changing. This can best be summarized using ratios. A 40-year trend is very revealing.

In Canada, the number of people in the support group (ages 18 to 64) will continue to increase until about 2021 and then will stabilize to the end of the forecast period (2031). For the United States, the number of supporters will continue to grow over the entire 40-year period.

At the beginning of the 1990s, there were 58 dependants for every 100 supporters in Canada, and 62 in the United States. The number of dependants per supporter is forecast to decline over the next two decades in both countries and then begin to rise rapidly thereafter as seniors become more prominent. Canada has a lower total ratio in each of the years shown below.

Now is the time to prepare for the sharp upturn forecast in the more distant future.

DEPENDENCY RATIOS
(dependants per 100 persons of working age [18 to 64])

	Canada 1991/2011/2031			**United States** 1990/2010/2030		
Total (0-17 plus 65+):	58	57	73	62*	61*	78*
- youth (0-17)	40	34	35	42*	39*	42*
- seniors (65+)	18	23*	38*	20*	22	36

* Indicates which country has the highest ratio for years shown.

Sources: Statistics Canada, special tabulation for the author. U.S. Bureau of the Census, Statistical Abstracts of the United States and Current Population Report P25-1092.

32/WOMEN OUTNUMBER MEN AS BOTH AGE

Females are more numerous than males in both Canada and the United States. Men start out ahead, but women have longer life expectancies in both countries.

Girl babies are less numerous than male babies. There are only 95 female babies born for every 100 male babies in both Canada and the United States. This ratio has remained stable for many years.

In Canada, the number of males continues to be larger than the number of females up to the age of 22, when women catch up. The Canadian male/female difference does not become very significant until the age of 60, after which the number of females rises rapidly.

In the United States, men outnumber women until the age of 30. Beyond 30, the number of American women expands relative to the number of men.

Overall, there are 103 females for every 100 males in Canada, and 105 females for every 100 males in the United States.

FEMALES PER 100 MALES
BY AGE GROUP
1991 for Canada, 1990 for United States

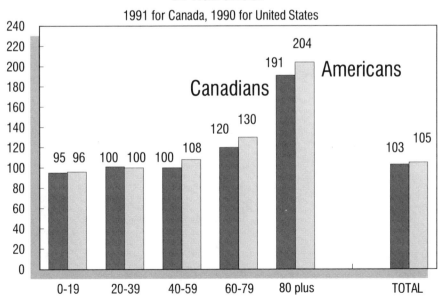

Sources: Statistics Canada, special tabulation for the author. U.S. Bureau of the Census, Statistical Abstracts of the United States and Current Population Report P25-1092.

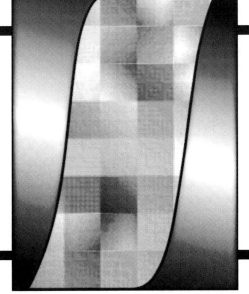

PART 7

MARRIAGE
AND
DIVORCE

THE "GOOD OLD DAYS" AND THE "GOOD NOWADAYS"

The proximity of Canada and the United States forces us to continue to interact with each other. The same cannot be said for relationships between couples in Canada and the United States.

When I was growing up, all of the adults around me seemed happily married. Everybody was married for life and appeared to be enjoying their relationships. The majority still do. My parents celebrated their 50th anniversary and renewed their wedding vows just a few years before my dad died of cancer. At the anniversary celebration, my body actually shook as I contrasted their married life with mine—I had divorced a few years earlier.

The image of marital happiness that I grew up with can be considered the "good old days." Paradoxically, for many people, divorce seems to open up the "good nowadays." I personally discovered a special freedom that has enriched my life, even though it disrupted the established relationship with my former partner and created an unwanted but temporary distancing with the teenagers I cared so much about. That is the dilemma—an image of happiness based on life-long couple relationships versus happiness based on individual freedom. For my generation, individual freedom is paramount. Building an enjoyable balance between the two is the ideal...I believe that I have both in my new relationship.

The current reality is one wherein people are less likely to marry at all, are increasingly likely to live in common-law relationships, and have a high divorce rate when they do marry. Canadian marriages last longer than they do in the United States. Canadian women stay divorced longer than American women, and longer than men in either country. Canadians maintain longer periods in common-law relationships. Americans live in more common-law relationships but for shorter periods of time.

What about the children of divorce? Specialists disagree on the ultimate impact of divorce on children. It is difficult to disagree with the idea that children should live in a happy family comprised of their two natural parents where they receive a lot of love and care, but the reality is often different. Other types of families can also provide this love and care.

One non-caring reality makes me angry. There are too many noncustodial parents who do not provide the family support they should (and have agreed to) pay. Do they want to make their own children suffer? Are they using their own children to get even with an ex-partner? To all of you who have had or will have children, please, it is your responsibility to both love and support them!

33/MARRIED LIFE LESS STABLE

"Till death us do part" does not carry the same life-time commitment it used to. Many relationships are not lasting.

Simple ratios can be used to summarize the underlying trends in marriage and divorce. The number of marriages per 100 persons aged 15 to 64 has been falling steadily for two decades in both Canada and the United States. The U.S. marriage rate is significantly higher than for Canada, and both are now the highest in the industrial world.

The number of divorces per 1,000 married women continues to rise for Canadians but may have flattened out or even declined for Americans. The American rate is still almost double the Canadian rate, and is the very highest among industrial countries.

The number of divorces now averages about 80,000 per year in Canada and about one million in the United States. In the mid-1980s, 28 per cent of Canadian marriages could be expected to end in divorce compared with 43 per cent for Americans. More recent data suggests that the Canadian rate could now be approaching 40 per cent.

MARRIAGE AND DIVORCE RATES

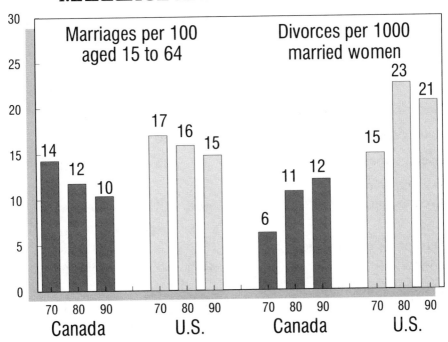

Sources: Statistics Canada, Catalogue 82-003, supplement # 17. U.S. Bureau of Labor Statistics, Monthly Economic Review, March 1990, and unpublished updates.

34/A CLOSER LOOK AT MARITAL RELATIONSHIPS

What is the probability you will ever marry? And, will it last? Some of the answers are different for Canadians and Americans.

The reply to these questions can get very complicated since people can get married, divorced, widowed, and then repeat it again two or more times. Analysts have developed what are called "marital status life tables" which track people through various marital stages and which attach probabilities to the occurrence of various stages for both Canadians and Americans.

Compared with Americans, Canadians have a similar likelihood of marrying: they get married at about the same age; marriages last about six years longer; the share of life lived as married is a bit higher; fewer marriages end in divorce; divorces last longer for Canadian women; fewer Canadian women re-marry and more are likely to be currently cohabiting.

More recent trends suggest that some of these differences have been reduced given that Canadian divorce rates have risen since the mid-1980s while American divorce rates have fallen slightly.

MARRIAGE AND DIVORCE COMPARISONS

	Canada 1984-86		United States 1988	
	Men	Women	Men	Women
Marriage				
Percentage who ever marry:	83%	86%	82%	87%
Average age at first marriage:	28	26	28	25
Average years of a marriage:	32	31	25	25
Percentage of life lived as married:	48%	43%	45%	41%
Divorce				
Percentage of marriages ending in divorce:	28%	28%	43%	43%
Average years' duration of a divorce:	8	16	8	13

	Remarriage			
Percentage of widowed who remarry:	14%	5%	17%	6%
Percentage of divorced who remarry:	76%	64%	78%	72%

	Cohabitation	
	Women (18-49)	Women (15-44)
Percentage presently cohabitating:	9% ('90)	5%
Percentage of married who ever cohabitated:	34% ('90)	40%

Sources: Statistics Canada, Catalogue 84-536. U.S. Bureau of the Census, Current Population Report P23-180. Robert Schoen and Robin Weinick, 1993, "The Slowing Metabolism of Marriage: Figures from 1988 U.S. Marital Status Life Tables." In *Demography,* Vol. 30 (No. 4), November 1993.

35/GETTING MARRIED AGAIN

High divorce rates are supporting the marriage market. The latest data suggests that Canadian women who marry will marry about 1.3 times over a lifetime compared to 1.6 for American women.

Remarriages now constitute almost one out of every four marriages in Canada, and they continue to form an increasing share of all marriages. The ratio of remarriages is much higher in the United States where about half of all marriages include one or more partners who have been married before. The trend seems to have stabilized for Americans.

Among Canadians, remarriages comprise the majority of all marriages beginning at 32 years of age for brides and 34 years for grooms. For Americans, this occurs about two years earlier.

Remarriages are high, even if more males and females choose not to officially remarry after divorce or widowhood. A growing proportion of divorced and widowed persons are choosing to live in common-law relationships. The percentage of couples who are currently cohabitating in Canada is about twice as high as in the United States.

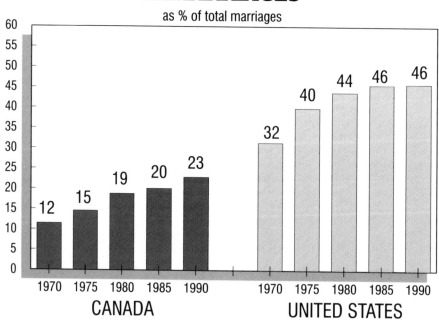

REMARRIAGES

as % of total marriages

Sources: Statistics Canada, Catalogue 82-003, supplement # 16. U.S. Bureau of the Census, Statistical Abstracts of the United States.

36/NUCLEAR HOUSEHOLDS ARE NO LONGER THE NORM

Childless couples plus one-person households are now the majority.

The nuclear family has traditionally been described as being made up of a husband, a wife and children living at home. During the early 1970s, about half of all Canadian households fit this nuclear definition, but only 30 per cent now do so. American households have experienced a similar trend; now, about one-quarter of households now fit the description of a nuclear family. Married couples without children now outnumber nuclear families in both countries. The upcoming boom in empty-nesters will increase the significance of this group.

Single-parent families are on the increase in both countries.

One-person households now form about one-quarter of all households in Canada and the United States. This household group is comprised of young people—and separated and divorced persons without children—and rapidly growing senior population. Over the next few decades, the anticipated growth in the number of seniors will cause the number of one-person households to swell even more.

HOUSEHOLDS BY TYPE

% distribution

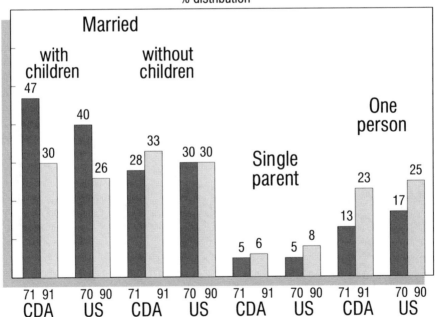

Note: Percentages do not total 100 because a category, "Other Unclassified Households," is not included.

Source: U.S. Bureau of Labor Statistics, Monthly Economic Review, March 1990. Census, Statistical Abstracts of the United States.

*THE
SCHOOL-
HOUSE*

GO TO SCHOOL—
AND WIN!

Young people in Canada and the United States are told that they must get a good education to succeed in life. They should listen and believe. The payoff is real. Older people should also listen and upgrade their skills.

Improve your odds for success. The more education you get, the better off you will be.

In my first book, *Canadian People Patterns,* I addressed the link between education, income and unemployment. It clearly showed that higher education leads to an improved standard of living for individuals. This chapter reiterates and updates this positive conclusion. I received several requests for permission to use that material in schools and newsletters; its popularity suggests that many people still need to be convinced about the positives of education.

Why are so many young people skeptical about the link between education and improved individual well-being? I suggest that the media should share part of the blame. The media frequently like to exaggerate the unemployment picture by searching out unemployed Ph.D.s in obscure fields who cannot find jobs in their own profession. These examples supposedly refute the argument that education is worthwhile. They do not! They point out exceptions rather than the norm. These stories may, however, suggest that vocational guidance counsellors and the whole education system need a lot of improvement.

Canadians and Americans support very expensive education systems compared to other countries in the industrial world. Even so, international testing indicates that both Canadian and American students earn very low ratings in mathematics and science. This suggests that, in an international context, the taxpayers in both countries are not getting as much value for their money. (Is this a source of skepticism about the value of education?) Education programs that are the most expensive in the industrial world do not automatically guarantee us an ability to be able to compete globally.

The school system should go beyond technical training and provide a stronger background on the people, team and group skills required to build strong individuals and organizations.

I want to repeat a question I asked in Chapter 6. What are older workers doing to keep ahead of the more educated workforce which is hot on their heels? Are they updating their intellectual capital in order to remain productive? They had better.

37/CANADIANS AND AMERICANS RECEIVE EXPENSIVE EDUCATIONS

Canadian and American taxpayers support the costliest formal education systems in the industrial world.

The Centre for Educational Research and Innovation of the OECD (Organization for Economic Co-operation and Development) found that Canada allocates 7.4 per cent of its total economic output to public and private education. This compares to 7.0 per cent in the United States and 5.0 per cent in Japan. (Japan has the least expensive system in the industrial world.) Canada has fewer students per teacher in both primary and secondary schools than does the United States.

Educational attainment is lower in Canada—17 per cent of the population aged 25 to 64 have a university degree compared to 24 per cent in the United States. More Canadians attend non-university colleges after high school (community colleges in Canada and "associate degrees" in the U.S. are prime examples).

Using OECD definitions, current graduation rates for secondary schools are similar in both countries while university graduation rates are a bit higher in Canada.

Both countries produce about the same percentage of university graduates with degrees in the sciences. This measure illustrates the capacity of an educational system to educate people in subjects that require rigorous training.

EDUCATION INDICATORS – 1991

	Canada	United States
Public/private education expenditures as a percentage of total economy:	7.4%	7.0%
Public/private expenditure per student (U.S. dollars):	$6,191	$6,593
Pupils per teacher ratio:		
-Primary schools	16.6 ('89)	17.5 ('89)
-Secondary schools	15.3 ('89)	15.8 ('89)
Educational attainment of population aged 25 to 64:		
-Some or all primary school	12%	7%
-Some secondary school	13%	10%
-Secondary school graduate	36%	47%

-Non-university (post s.s.)	23%	13%
-University graduate	17%	24%
Secondary school graduation rate:	73%	74%
University graduation rate:	33%	30%
Percentage of university graduates in natural sciences, maths, computers, and engineering:	16%	15%

Sources: Organization for Economic Co-operation and Development, Education at a Glance, 1992 and 1993.

38/INTERNATIONAL TESTING REVEALS POOR RANKINGS

It is relatively easy to measure the number of graduates and the cost of the educational system. It is more difficult to gauge the quality of the results. An educational system should produce a competitive workforce plus provide the basis for personal growth and development.

International comparisons of student abilities have been prepared on an occasional basis. The International Assessment of Educational Progress project tested 13-year-old mathematics and science students in 15 countries in 1991.

Canadian mathematics students correctly answered 62 per cent of questions compared to 55 per cent for American students. Canadian science students also did a bit better in the sciences by correctly answering 69 per cent of the questions compared to 67 per cent for American students.

In both categories, Canada ranked ninth and the United States ranked 13th among the 15 countries surveyed. Caution is advised in interpreting these rankings given some allowances for inconsistencies in the selection of student participants.

INDICATORS FOR 13-YEAR-OLD STUDENT PARTICIPANTS IN INTERNATIONAL ASSESSEMENT OF EDUCATIONAL PROGRESS TESTS – 1991

	Canadians	Americans
Days of instruction per year:	188	178
Mathematics Students		
Per cent correct answers:	62%	55%
Minutes of instruction per week:	225	228
Percentage of students with 2 hours or more of homework per day:	27%	29%
Science Students		
Per cent correct answers:	69%	67%
Minutes of instruction per week:	156	233
Percentage of students with 2 hours or more of homework per day:	26%	31%
Percentage of students who watch television 5 hours or more per day:	15%	22%

Sources: Organization for Economic Co-operation and Development, *Education at a Glance,* 1992 and 1993. Michael Wolff, *Where We Stand.* New York: Bantam Books, 1992. International Association for the Evaluation of Education Achievement, 1992.

39/EDUCATION MEANS LESS UNEMPLOYMENT

Society gets a payoff from education. Individuals also benefit in additional job security.

One of the clear benefits of education is an increased probability of being able to find and maintain jobs. An Organization for Economic Co-operation and Development (OECD) project studied the links between education and unemployment among industrial countries. In total terms, Canada has a higher overall unemployment rate than does the United States. This has been the new reality throughout most of the last decade.

Unemployment clearly declines as education increases. As a group, persons with all or part of a primary school education had a rate of unemployment of 14.6 per cent in Canada and 11.8 per cent in the United States in 1991. In Canada, the rate declined to 9.5 per cent for secondary school graduates, to 7.8 per cent for those with non-university higher education, and to about 5 per cent for university graduates. The pattern for the United States is identical but the figures are lower in all cases. The link between higher education and lower unemployment is true for both men and women.

UNEMPLOYMENT RATE % BY EDUCATION
PERSONS AGED 25-64, 1991

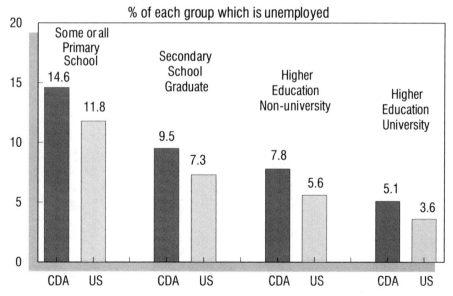

Sources: Organization for Economic Co-operation and Development, *Education at a Glance,* 1992 and 1993.

40/HIGHER EDUCATION LEADS TO HIGHER INDIVIDUAL EARNINGS

Parents tell their children to get a good education. An OECD study covering 1990 clearly demonstrates the positive monetary impact of additional education.

In Canada, a person aged 25 to 64 with all or part of a primary school education had earnings equal to 80 per cent of the earnings of a secondary school graduate. An American with a primary school education earned about 70 per cent of what a secondary school graduate earned. Secondary school graduation seems to be more necessary in the United States.

University graduates in Canada and the United States had earnings 56 per cent to 69 per cent higher than a secondary school graduate. This points to a very large individual payoff over a lifetime of work.

A university degree pays an even bigger premium for women than for men. A 45- to 64-year-old Canadian female with a university degree earns 65 per cent more than a female with a secondary school diploma compared to a 54 per cent gain among men.

AVERAGE* EARNINGS BY EDUCATION
PERSONS AGED 25-64, 1990

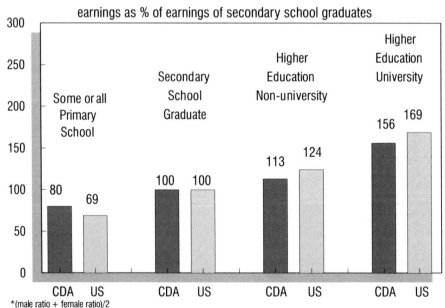

earnings as % of earnings of secondary school graduates

*(male ratio + female ratio)/2

Sources: Organization for Economic Co-operation and Development, *Education at a Glance,* 1992 and 1993.

WORKING FOR A LIVING

SEARCHING FOR ENJOYABLE WORK

The desire to work to provide for ourselves and our families is deeply rooted in our collective mindset. People not only want to work to earn money, but they also want to have fun when they work. I know I do.

The job market is changing rapidly. Globalization, rationalization, communication, education, and a whole bunch of other "-ations" are transforming the world of work. "Lifers" are becoming rare in the workplace. Entitlement to a specific job over a lifetime is dead.

Unpaid family work is on the way out. Just look at many teenagers—they now want real money to help around the house. It is somewhat ironic , even if it makes good economic sense, that more and more adults now get paid to work for others and then find that it is necessary to hire someone to do the work at home that they no longer have the time—or inclination—to do themselves. Earning our own money (and controlling it) is now a key driver for many of our business and personal activities.

Self-employment and second job trends point in part to an increasing demand to do enjoyable work. The expression "do what you love and the money will follow" is becoming more popular. Work and enjoyment are not mutually exclusive. Surveys suggest that two-thirds of workers would actually like to own their own business, and those who actually follow through report greater overall satisfaction from their jobs than do employees. This tendency is one of the reasons that part-time jobs are growing in importance; many workers want the flexibility. The aging of the workforce, coupled with many more empty nesters, will provide more opportunities and flexibility for self-employment. Of course, many people pursue self-employment because they are not able to get that full-time job they really want.

I frequently tell governments and bankers that their growth and lending policies reflect the outdated concept that "Services are no good(s)." For far too long, governments and bankers have hung onto a belief that the only really good jobs are in the goods-producing sector. This notion should be replaced by "Services are good(s)." Did you know that the fastest growth in foreign investment and world trade is attributable to services?

Progress for Canadians and Americans needs to be measured by the degree to which we get happiness from both our work and our leisure activities. Happy work and happy holidays!

41/MORE CANADIANS TYPICALLY IN THE LABOUR FORCE

Are you working? Are you looking for work? If so, then you are part of the labour force of your country.

"Participation rates" measure the percentage of persons of working age who are in the labour force. Canadian data collectors assume that the working age begins at 15, while in the United States it is set at 16 years of age. This difference does not alter overall trends. In both countries, persons could potentially be part of the labour force until deceased.

During the 1980s, a higher percentage of Canadians were in the labour force than were Americans. The rising participation rate in both countries reflected a declining participation by men, which was more than offset by a rapid increase in the participation of women. The recession of the early 1990s caused a much sharper drop in participation rates in Canada than in the United States—both rates are moving up again as the economic recovery continues.

LABOUR FORCE PARTICIPATION RATES

% of working age persons in workforce

Sources: Statistics Canada, Catalogue 71-220. U.S. Bureau of the Census, Statistical Abstracts of the United States and Bureau of Labor Statistics, Employment and Earnings.

42/MAJORITY OF WOMEN ARE NOW IN PAID LABOUR FORCE

Men are still more likely to be part of the paid labour force than women, but women are quickly narrowing the gap. Government statistics do not include housework—by women or men—as part of the workforce.

In 1980, about 78 per cent of Canadian men of working age were in the labour force as were an almost identical percentage of American men. The rate of participation fell in both countries. It is noteworthy that the decline in male participation was apparent in all age groups in both countries.

Approximately half of all women of working age were in the paid labour force in 1980, and exactly 58 per cent in both countries by 1993. The increase resulted from labour force changes among all women aged 25 and over. Currently, a women aged 45 to 64 is almost as likely to be in the paid labour force as is a women under the age of 25. Women are entering and staying in the workforce.

PARTICIPATION RATES BY AGE AND SEX
(percentage of each age group in labour force)

	Canadians 1980/1993/Change	Americans 1980/1993/Change
MEN		
Total:	78% 73% -5	77% 76% -1
Under 25:	78% 66% -12	74% 70% -4
25-44:	96% 92% -4	95% 94% -1
45-64:	85% 77% -8	82% 80% -2
65+:	15% 10% -5	19% 16% -3
WOMEN		
Total:	50% 58% +8	52% 58% +6
Under 25:	63% 61% -2	62% 62% —
25-44:	62% 77% +15	66% 75% +9
45-64:	45% 57% +12	52% 62% +10
65+:	4% 4% —	8% 8% —

Sources: Statistics Canada, Catalogue 71-220. U.S. Bureau of the Census, Statistical Abstracts of the United States and Bureau of Labor Statistics, Employment and Earnings.

43/MORE WORKING MOTHERS AND DUAL-INCOME FAMILIES

Mothers with young children are returning from maternity leave to work sooner. Dual-income families are now the norm in both countries.

During the early 1980s, fewer than half of mothers with pre-school children (under age six) were working outside the home. About 60 per cent of this group of mothers are now in the paid labour force in each country. In Canada, mothers with working spouses are more likely to be working outside the home. In the U.S., single mothers are more likely to be employed externally.

Today, about three-quarters of mothers with children aged six to 15 or 17 are working outside the home. This represents a significant increase in participation compared to a decade earlier.

For the majority of husband/wife families, both partners are now in the workforce. The stereotype of a working husband with a wife at home has been the minority situation for more than two decades.

LABOUR FORCE PARTICIPATION BY MOTHERS
(percentage of each group in labour force)

	Canadians 1981/1993		Americans 1980/1990	
Mothers by age of youngest child:				
- pre-school (0-5):	48%	63%	47%	58%
- 6-15 (Canada)/6-17 (U.S.):	61%	76%	64%	75%

HUSBAND/WIFE FAMILIES BY NUMBER OF EARNERS

	Canadians 1980/1991		Americans 1980/1990	
Both in labour force:	51%	61%	46%	54%
Single-income earner:	38%	24%	39%	29%
No income earner:	11%	15%	15%	17%

Sources: Statistics Canada, Catalogue 71-220, 13-215. U.S. Bureau of the Census, Statistical Abstracts of the United States and Bureau of Labor Statistics, Employment and Earnings.

44/EXPANDING WORKFORCES IN BOTH COUNTRIES

The size of the labour force has increased at about the same pace in both Canada and the United States.

The number of persons who are 15 or 16 years of age and over (the source population), multiplied by the percentage of this group who are or want to work, makes up the total labour force in each country. These include persons who are employed plus those who are unemployed but actively looking for work. In 1993, about 14 million Canadians and 128 million Americans were in the labour force.

In Canada, there were 121 people in the labour force in 1993 for every 100 in the labour force in 1980, an increase just above the American advance (120). The steady increase in workforces slowed only a bit during the recent recession. Only Australia, among the top-10 industrial countries, enjoyed a more rapid rate of growth in its labour force over the entire period than did Canada and the United States.

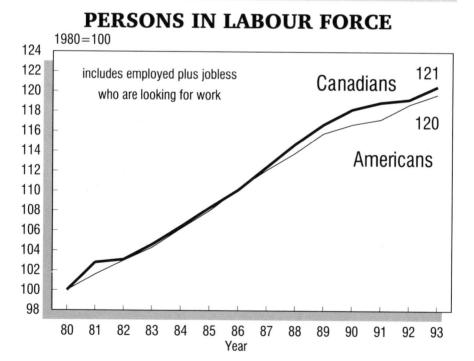

PERSONS IN LABOUR FORCE

1980=100

includes employed plus jobless who are looking for work

Canadians 121

Americans 120

Year

Sources: Statistics Canada, Catalogue 71-220. U.S. Bureau of the Census, Statistical Abstracts of the United States and Bureau of Labor Statistics, Employment and Earnings.

45/CANADIAN JOBS DIP MORE DURING RECESSION

Jobs! Jobs! Jobs! The growth in the number of people who are working is one of the best measures of success for a country.

In 1993, there were 116 Canadians at work for every 100 who were working in 1980. The United States created more jobs over the same period with 120 jobs in place in 1993 for every 100 jobs in 1980. This caused the Canadian unemployment rate to worsen sharply relative to the United States. (The next chapter takes a closer look at unemployment.)

Canadian jobs declined more sharply during both of the latest recessions. The level of Canadian employment dipped sharply in 1982 and did not surpass pre-recession levels until 1985. The expansion then produced steady growth to 1990. The early 1990s' recession was also worse in Canada with large job losses during both 1991 and 1992. A recovery is now underway. It is clear that Canadian jobs were much more sensitive to the last two economic downturns.

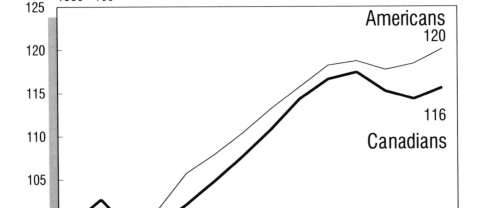

PERSONS WITH JOBS

Sources: Statistics Canada, Catalogue 71-220. U.S. Bureau of the Census, Statistical Abstracts of the United States and Bureau of Labor Statistics, Employment and Earnings.

46/CANADIAN WOMEN SPUR JOB GROWTH

Women have been entering the workforce in record numbers and have been successful in finding jobs.

There were 133 Canadian women working in 1993 for every 100 working in 1980. This enormous increase is only a bit larger than the advance for American women (130). The progression for women generated an unemployment rate that is now lower than it is for men in both countries; this is the reverse of the situation in 1980.

The current situation for Canadian men is rather dismal—up only 5 per cent in 1993 relative to the beginning of the period. Job growth among American men was a bit better than the Canadian experience—113 men working in 1993 for every 100 at work in 1980.

Women's share of all jobs increased to 46 per cent in both countries. Contrary to popular belief, women's share of full-time jobs rose during this period to 41 per cent; their share of part-time jobs remained steady.

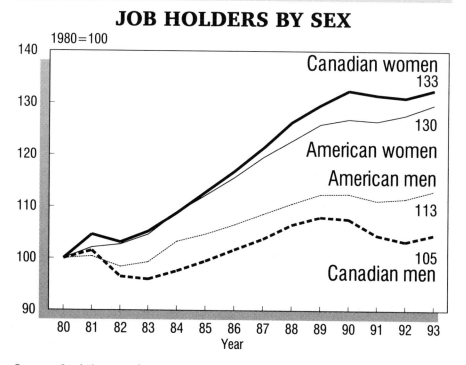

JOB HOLDERS BY SEX

Sources: Statistics Canada, Catalogue 71-220. U.S. Bureau of the Census, Statistical Abstracts of the United States and Bureau of Labor Statistics, Employment and Earnings.

47/PART-TIME JOBS SOAR IN CANADA

Full-time or part-time? The trends in Canada and the United States are different, but they end up at the same place. Confused? Read on!

Statistics Canada classifies full-timers as those people who work 30 hours or more in a week. American numbers have been adjusted here to make them compatible with the Canadian definition. American statisticians typically use 35 hours as the cut-off point between the two types of jobs.

The number of full-time jobs in Canada increased by only 8 per cent from 1980 to 1993, while the number of part-time jobs soared by over 50 per cent. In the United States, the rate of growth was more even—full-time and part-time jobs increased by about 20 to 25 per cent respectively.

Shame on Canada? This conclusion may be unfair as the share of all jobs which were classified as part-time stood at exactly 17 per cent in both countries at the end of the period. It seems that Canada merely caught up with the American situation.

GROWTH IN FULL- AND PART-TIME JOBS
1980 TO 1993

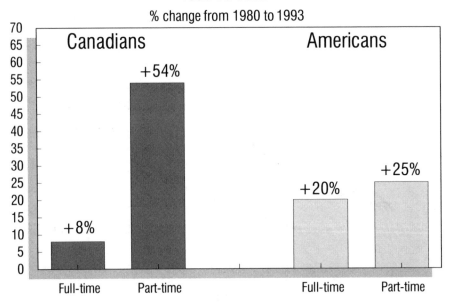

Sources: Statistics Canada, Catalogue 71-220. U.S. Bureau of the Census, Statistical Abstracts of the United States and Bureau of Labor Statistics, Employment and Earnings.

48/CANADIAN WOMEN LEAD BOOM IN SELF-EMPLOYMENT

More and more employees say they want to be their own bosses—take this job and shove it! It is becoming a reality for more people. Layoffs are forcing some people to move to self-employment.

The number of self-employed Canadians increased by about 40 per cent between 1981 and 1993. The biggest jump was among Canadian women—an 83 per cent increase compared to a 28 per cent expansion for Canadian men. The same gender-specific trends are evident for Americans with self-employment for women up by 38 per cent and 11 per cent for men.

Agricultural self-employment declined in both countries. Self-employment figures advanced in both the goods-producing and service sectors in each country.

By 1993, about 15 per cent of workers in Canada and 10 per cent of workers in the United States were operating their own businesses. The self-employed plus employees in small firms were the source of all net new jobs in both countries during the last decade and even longer, and that trend will continue. Big companies are important but they will not be the direct source of new jobs. At best they will only manage to maintain current job levels.

GROWTH IN SELF-EMPLOYMENT
1981 TO 1993

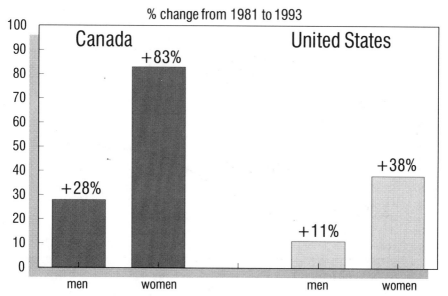

Sources: Statistics Canada, Catalogue 71-220. U.S. Bureau of the Census, Statistical Abstracts of the United States and Bureau of Labor Statistics, Employment and Earnings.

49/A SECOND JOB IS MORE POPULAR FOR AMERICANS

Need to reduce debt, or perhaps you just enjoy working on a second job? Canadians and Americans are moonlighting more than ever before.

In 1992, some 600,000 Canadians and 7.2 million Americans were working at second jobs. Since the early 1980s, increases are evident in both countries, even though the recent recession reduced the number of second jobs that were available. Over 6 per cent of Americans now hold a second job, and about 5 per cent of Canadians are doing the same.

In the past, Canadian men were much more likely to have a second job than were women. This changed in the 1980s with Canadian women now being just a bit more likely to have a second job than are men. (Many women would claim that they already hold down two jobs if housework is included.)

In the United States, women have virtually doubled their rate of moonlighting but still lag behind the rate for men. The difference will disappear in a very few years.

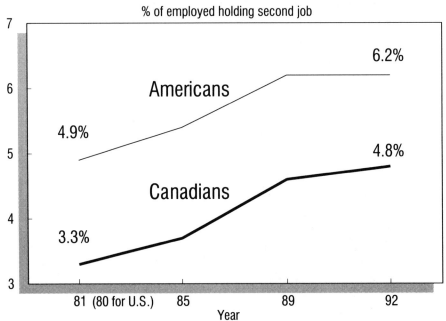

EMPLOYEE MOONLIGHTING
% of employed holding second job

Sources: Statistics Canada, Catalogue 71-220. U.S. Bureau of the Census, Statistical Abstracts of the United States and Bureau of Labor Statistics, Employment and Earnings.

50/SERVICES PROVIDE ALL NET NEW JOBS

Service employment has been getting a bad rap. In an information and knowledge age, a healthy service industry is driving progress and job growth.

Don't depend on a growing number of jobs in the goods-producing sector. In 1993, 3.3 million Canadians were employed in the goods-producing sector, down from 3.6 million in 1980. A similar decline occurred in the United States, and the trend will continue.

All of the new jobs created in both countries are in service industries. The same is true for other industrialized countries. The number of service jobs in Canada grew by over 25 per cent from 1980 to 1993. In the United States, the growth was even higher, advancing by one-third. About three-quarters of all jobs in both countries are now in services.

As a general rule, but not always, service jobs pay less than goods- producing jobs. The lowest paid are in traditional services such as retailing, some positions in hospitals, restaurants and travel agencies. Higher-paying service jobs are found in transportation, communications, finance, real estate and business service companies.

SERVICE JOBS' SHARE

service jobs as % of all jobs

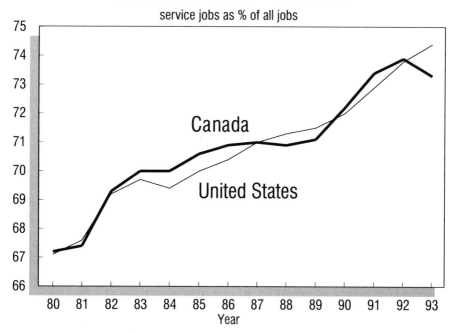

Sources: Statistics Canada, Catalogue 71-220. U.S. Bureau of the Census, Statistical Abstracts of the United States and Bureau of Labor Statistics, Employment and Earnings.

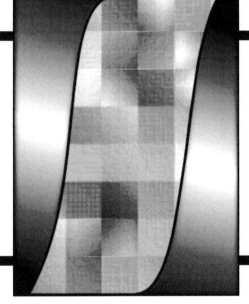

NOT
WORKING
FOR A
LIVING

FIGHTING JOBLESSNESS IN CANADA

I don't like the "new" Canadian unemployment situation described in this chapter. The findings go a long way towards explaining why Canadians are not satisfied with the direction the country is going.

During the 1980s and so far in the 1990s, Canada's unemployment rate has been much higher than in the United States. This trend stands in sharp contrast to the situation during the previous two decades.

Certain politicians and analysts tell us that unemployment is higher now due to international factors. They claim we are part of a worldwide restructuring trend. The United States is also restructuring but the U.S. has been able to do so with comparatively less unemployment.

Why is Canadian unemployment much higher than in the United States?

The Canadian economy was hit very hard by the recession of the early 1980s—it was the deepest economic decline since the great depression and hit our commodity-based sectors the hardest. Over the remainder of the 1980s and into the early 1990s, the economy was held back by a combination of a frequently over-valued dollar, a generally high interest rate policy, and the untimely introduction of the Goods and Services Tax in 1991. The GST is a much better tax than the manufacturer's sales tax it replaced—but it was introduced at an unfortunate time. Canadian immigration was also too high in the late 1980s, the early 1990s, and continues to be so.

The Canada-United States Free Trade deal definitely caused some restructuring, but its impact was probably not negative in overall employment terms. The restructuring was necessary in any case. We must be able to compete.

A lower Canadian dollar and interest rates more in line with the United States should help narrow the unemployment gap over the next few years. Reducing unemployment must be a key policy objective. The governor of The Bank of Canada must be a team player. If he or she is not, they should be replaced. At the same time, all levels of government must commit themselves to lowering and eliminating their deficits.

Canada needs to re-examine its unemployment insurance scheme to improve worker mobility and training. Workers in depressed areas should be encouraged to move. Mobility and flexibility in general must be encouraged. Workers must accept the view that unrealistic wage demands will in time lead to more unemployment.

I believe that Canada should reduce immigration for the next two years, and then open it up again as unemployment levels become more respectable. In the longer term, immigration will need to be even higher than in the past to help offset the expected flattening out of Canada's labour force growth over the next decade. I also believe that immigrants should be selected based primarily on Canada's economic and labour force needs—and the biggest need will be for young workers who possess the skills demanded by a rapidly changing economy.

51/CANADIANS SUFFER MORE UNEMPLOYMENT IN DECADE

Joblessness reduces both output and the demand for the goods and services that lost incomes would otherwise generate. Unemployment represents hardship for many. It is the most talked about and reported economic indicator.

Canadian and American unemployment rates have traditionally tracked along with each other very closely. During the 1960s and '70s, the jobless rate averaged 5.9 per cent in Canada and 5.5 per cent in the United States. This close relationship was still evident as both countries entered the early 1980s.

Something very different happened during the rest of the 1980s and into the early '90s. Even though the trend in Canadian joblessness mirrored shifts in the American rate, the spread between them has widened dramatically. During 1993, the Canadian rate was more than 4 percentage points higher than in the United States. The key factor behind this widening spread is the slower rate of job creation in Canada, at a time when an almost identical increase in the number of persons entering the workforce is evident in both countries.

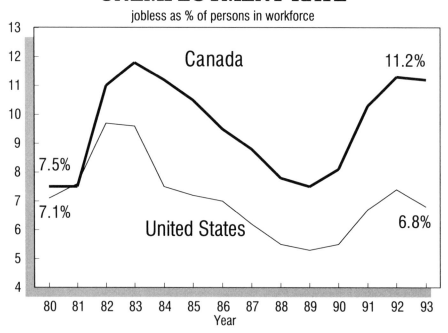

UNEMPLOYMENT RATE
jobless as % of persons in workforce

Sources: Statistics Canada, Catalogue 71-220. U.S. Bureau of the Census, Statistical Abstracts of the United States and Bureau of Labor Statistics, Employment and Earnings.

52/CANADIAN JOBLESSNESS RISES FASTER BY MOST MEASURES

By all yardsticks, a much higher percentage of people are now looking for work in Canada than in the United States. On the other hand, similar percentages of people seem discouraged.

The "official" unemployment rate for Canada was similar (7.5 per cent) to the American rate (7.1 per cent) in the early 1980s, but it rose sharply above the American rate during the remainder of the period. For each of the rates shown below, except one, the Canadian rate is now decisively above the corresponding American rate.

American unemployment rates improved for American females and youth.

The most rapid increase in rates in both countries was among the long-term unemployed (13 weeks or more), with the rate more than doubling in Canada and increasing by over 40 per cent in the United States. It seems peculiar that the statistics indicate little change in both countries in the rate of discouraged persons who are no longer looking and have dropped out of the workforce. In Canada, the overall rate for males jumped by 70 per cent while the rate for all adults soared by over 80 per cent.

ALTERNATIVE UNEMPLOYMENT RATES

	Canada		United States	
	1980	1993	1980	1993
Official rate:	7.5%	11.2%	7.1%	6.8%
RATES BY DURATION				
Long-term unemployed (13 weeks or more):	2.5%	5.6%	1.7%	2.4%
Persons who are discouraged and have dropped out of the workforce:	1.0%	0.9%	0.9%	0.9%
RATES BY SEX AND AGE				
Male workers:	6.9%	11.7%	6.9%	7.1%
Female workers:	8.4%	10.6%	7.4%	6.5%
Adult (25+) workers:	5.4%	9.9%	5.1%	5.6%
Youth (under 25) workers:	13.8%	17.7%	13.8%	13.3%

Sources: Statistics Canada, Catalogue 71-220 and unpublished data. U.S. Bureau of Labor Statistics, Monthly Economic Review, March 1990, and published updates.

53/YOUTH ARE CLOSING THE GAP

The number of young people of labour force age have declined during the last dozen years. This trend has in reality improved their status relative to the overall category of male adult wage earners.

The size of the youth labour force (under 25 years) shrank by about 18 per cent since 1980 in both Canada and the United States, while the number of males over the age of 25 increased rapidly.

Opposing trends in the number of workers available in each age group has translated into a relative improvement in unemployment prospects for youth in Canada. During the early 1980s, the unemployment rate for Canadian youth was 2.8 times the unemployment rate for males 25 and older—by 1993 the youth rate was only 1.8 times the rate for adult males.

In the United States, the ratio of youth unemployment to adult male unemployment declined from 2.9 in 1980 to 2.3 in 1993.

It seems that the relative shortage of young people is indeed putting them in a more positive position relative to older male workers. Media reports do not seem to be aware of this trend. More of their stories should focus on the difficult situation being faced by adult men.

YOUTH VS ADULT MEN JOBLESS RATES
ratio of youth rate to rate for men 25+

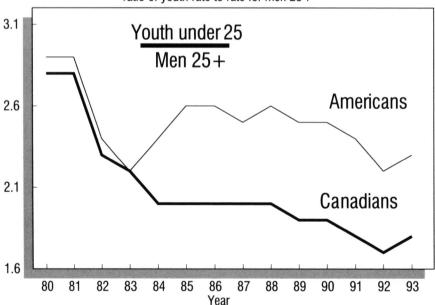

Sources: Statistics Canada, Catalogue 71-220. U.S. Bureau of the Census, Statistical Abstracts of the United States and Bureau of Labor Statistics, Employment and Earnings.

54/PUBLIC EMPLOYMENT AGENCIES ARE LOSING GROUND

The vast majority of unemployed persons are actively looking for work, and they are using more than one technique.

Some 95 per cent of unemployed Canadians were actively looking for jobs in 1993. This high search percentage reflects the fact that the unemployed can no longer depend on being recalled to their old jobs. A comparable ratio is not available for the United States.

Contacting employers directly is the most popular method of job search in both Canada and the United States, though it's a method that seems to be losing some of its appeal in Canada.

Placing or checking ads has now become the number two approach to finding jobs in both countries.

Although governments are suggesting that people keep in touch with a public employment agency to find new jobs, a declining number are making use of this service. Currently, about one-third of unemployed Canadians and less than one-quarter of unemployed Americans make use of public employment agencies. This suggests a need for re-thinking the role of these agencies.

JOB SEARCH METHODS OF UNEMPLOYED

	Canadians 1980/1993	**Americans** 1980/1993
Contact employers directly:	72% 68%	73% 73%
Check or use advertisements:	39% 59%	31% 42%
Use public employment agency:	51% 37%	28% 22%

Sources: Statistics Canada, Catalogue 71-220. U.S. Bureau of the Census, Statistical Abstracts of the United States and Bureau of Labor Statistics, Employment and Earnings.

JOB
FUTURES

JOB FUTURES
AND YOU

The future is basically unpredictable. The best result that economic forecasters can hope for is to provide some rough idea of the general direction that the economy is headed and what that means for jobs.

Detailed job forecasts usually begin by establishing one or more scenarios regarding the outlook for the overall economy. Will the economy grow rapidly, slowly or moderately? The United States Department of Labor prepares three different scenarios but allocates most of its write-up to describing the middle scenario. Only one scenario is prepared in Canada. Before deciding on its final version, the Canadian forecast is reviewed by industry and government groups. The end result is a detailed forecast of activity at the industry level with "some" credibility relative to general direction.

The next step in this mechanical process is to assess what kinds of occupations are needed to fill the demands within each of the industry groups. This is done by studying occupational trends within industries and tying these into the projected industry forecasts. This process provides general directions only. The methodology cannot capture major breakthroughs in technology which have before and will again greatly alter occupational demands. Even so, the forecasts serve a useful purpose by highlighting potential winners and losers on the occupational front.

These general forecasts, coupled with ongoing scanning of the latest occupational trends, can provide youth, mature workers and counsellors with a valuable view of the future work force.

Rapid changes in labour markets necessitate that workers must look beyond their current technical skills. They must develop effective personal behaviour traits; these include effective communication, thinking and learning, positive attitudes, responsibility, adaptability and teamwork. I believe that future success will depend as much on people skills as on technical skills.

In a more general sense, the work environment is no longer based on "entitlement." This means no coasting. People must take charge of their own careers rather than leaving themselves in the hands of their employers. This is a process that requires that individuals understand themselves, that they know what their passions are, that they accept the fact that jobs are events, not permanent structures, and that they practice life-long learning. Good luck on your learning journey!

55/EMPLOYMENT FORECASTS TO 2005

Long-term forecasts help highlight what might be done to achieve specified economic targets and to assess future job requirements.

An Occupational Projection System was used by Human Resources Development Canada to prepare forecasts out to the year 2005. The forecast, prepared in 1992, anticipates an annual growth of 163,000 jobs. This results in an unemployment rate still hovering around 10 per cent by 2005. Not very challenging! About 200,000 new jobs per year (an additional 37,000 per year) would be required to return to the unemployment rate of the early 1980s, and 225,000 new jobs would lower the rate to 5.5 per cent by 2005. This would compare with an annual growth of 219,000 jobs during the previous 15-year period.

The U.S. Department of Labor has prepared three scenarios. The "medium" scenario paints a picture wherein 1,641,000 jobs are created annually and unemployment falls to a respectable 5.5 per cent by 2005. The job creation rate was 2.1 million per year from 1975 to 1990. The other scenarios see unemployment adjusting within a range of 4.0 to 7.0 per cent by 2005.

FORECASTS OF JOB GROWTH AND UNEMPLOYMENT

	Annual Job Growth 1990-2005 (thousands)	Unemployment Rate 2005
Canada		
Canadian Occupational Projection System (COPS):	163	10.1%
Alternative assumption #1:*	200	7.5%
Alternative assumption #2:*	225	5.5%
United States		
U.S. Department of Labor:		
-Medium-growth scenario	1,641	5.5%
-High-growth scenario	2,131	4.0%
-Low-growth scenario	948	7.0%

*Author's calculations.

Sources: Human Resources Development Canada, Canadian Occupational Projection System, published and unpublished data, 1993. U.S. Bureau of Labor Statistics, Outlook 1990-2005.

56/ The "TOP 10" IN FUTURE JOB GROWTH

Students and human resources planners need to keep an eye open for those occupational opportunities for which demand will increase rapidly.

Economic and occupational forecasts are prepared by Human Resources Development Canada and the United States Department of Labor. The Canadian forecast and the medium-growth scenario for the United States make projections for about 500 detailed occupations, all of which have been ranked in terms of percentage growth from 1990 to 2005. The top 10 in each country are expected to expand in a range from 66 per cent to 100 per cent over the forecast period.

The fastest-growing occupations are generally in health, information technology and services in both countries.

Four of the 10 fastest-growing occupations in Canada are in the health area, while in the United States more than half of the top 10 relate to health care. Rapid advances are also projected for systems analysts, computer operators and operations research analysts. Within the top 10 in both countries, all but automobile fabricators fall within the service category.

10 FASTEST-GROWING OCCUPATIONS, 1990-2005
(ranked by percentage increase over period)

Canada	**United States**
Respiratory technicians	Home health aides
Systems analysts	Paralegals
Automobile fabricators and assemblers	Systems analysts and computer scientists
Occupational therapists	Personal and home care aides
Speech therapists	Physical therapists
Electronic data processor equipment operators	Medical assistants
Salespersons	Operations research analysts
Claims adjusters	Human services workers
Child care workers	Radiologic technologists and technicians
Dental hygienists	Medical secretaries

Sources: Human Resources Development Canada, Canadian Occupational Projection System, published and unpublished data, 1993. U.S. Bureau of Labor Statistics, Outlook 1990-2005.

57/OCCUPATIONS WITH FADING FUTURES

A lot of occupations have seen their best days! Long-term decline is in the forecasts by Human Resources Development Canada and the U.S. Department of Labor. For several occupational areas, job opportunities will shrink by 30 to 60 per cent between 1990 and 2005. Within the 500 American occupations studied, approximately one in four will experience declining job levels.

Most of the declining occupations are in the manufacturing sector—international competitiveness and imports are costing jobs in Canada and the United States. Office automation and new information technologies are pushing many skills into a "surplus." Other occupations have been shrinking as part of a long-term trend; railway conductors and directory-assistance operators are perfect examples.

In Canada, categories of work which are anticipated to experience the greatest declines are in tobacco processing and machine tool operations where half of the jobs may disappear. Contractions in the range of 60 per cent are projected for frame wirers and central-office operators in the United States.

10 OCCUPATIONS SHRINKING THE FASTEST 1990-2005
(ranked by percentage decline over period)

Canada	United States
Tobacco processing	Frame wirers, central office
Machine tool operators	Central office operators
Pressing	Directory assistance operators
Projectionists	Station installers and repairers, telephone
Wood machining	Electrical and electronic equipment operators, precision
Textile spinning	Shoe sewing machine operators and tenders
Railway conductors	Electrical and electronic assemblers
Fruit and vegetable canning	Central office and PBX installers
Paper products fabricators	Child care workers in private households
Cellulose pulp preparators	Signal and track switch operators

Sources: Human Resources Development Canada, Canadian Occupational Projection System, published and unpublished data, 1993. U.S. Bureau of Labor Statistics, Outlook 1990-2005.

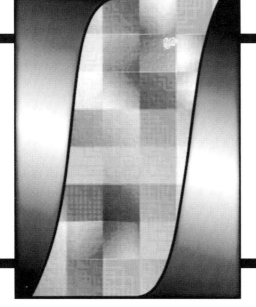

*WALLETS
AND
PURSES*

FLAT INCOMES AND A LOT OF INEQUALITY

There is no easy way to evaluate income levels, or to judge whether their distribution is fair or unfair. The drive to achieve higher individual and family incomes definitely motivates hard work and innovation, and is a major factor in stimulating national vitality. At the same time, I strongly believe that part of the aggregate income generated should be allocated in such a manner that poverty, especially among children and the elderly, is minimized.

Over the last decade, the real level of family and individual incomes has been relatively stagnant in both countries. Typically, Canadian and American families have not seen their economic situations improve since the outset of the 1980s. And this is a trend that is likely to continue for several more years as the impact of globalization and competition intensifies. (Sorry!)

The flat outlook for incomes and excessive government debt in both Canada and the United States will undoubtedly put stress on programs aimed at income redistribution. This will be particularly difficult among Americans because of the undeniable growth in inequality in that country during the last decade—trickle-down economics has produced a "sucking upwards" for the better off. Support for the less fortunate is much stronger and effective in Canada, but it will also come under attack. Hopefully, it will not lead to the income extremes evident in the United States. Canada's current income distribution is one of the key positive characteristics that differentiates Canadians from Americans.

Excessive government debt and high taxation, particularly in Canada, suggest that many long-standing government programs aimed at individuals and corporations should and will be closely scrutinized to both reduce spending and to reallocate funds to people who really need them. Many programs need to be refocused. Reducing inequalities, especially in the United States, must be a priority—too many Americans live in poverty and go without the basics of health care.

Can the United States use its "peace dividend" to help poor people? Can Canadians save money by constructing a more cost-effective educational system and by modernizing the unemployment insurance scheme? It is time to tackle the "sacred cows" in order to make them more effective. Many old programs need new faces. Some may need to disappear.

The public needs to become less skeptical of honest politicians; conversely, many politicians should also clean up their act and focus on the needs of people rather than wealthy pressure groups. The general public, cannot afford to continuously denounce and destroy good and honest leaders and politicians who are working to build a stronger and fairer system. We are all in this together. We—individuals, business, labour groups, government and volunteer organizations—must become more open to constructive change that reflects the new realities.

58/PRICES MOVED UP FASTER FOR CANADIANS

Trying to keep track of rising prices? Canadians have had a tougher time during the last decade.

Government price checkers are out every month recording the latest prices for a typical consumer basket comprised of goods and services that people buy for everyday living. The results are published and widely reported a few weeks later.

Consumer prices in Canada rose by 94 per cent from 1980 to 1993. In the United States, they advanced by 76 per cent. Canadian prices started the 1980s with a blast—they advanced by 10 to 12 per cent per year until 1982 and then slowed within a range of 4 to 6 per cent until 1991. Prices in 1992, 1993 and 1994 rose by less than 2 per cent, the slowest rate of increase in 30 years. American consumer prices increased less quickly during nine of the 13 years following 1980. In 1993, American prices advanced by 3 per cent.

Over the entire period, Canadian prices advanced faster than U.S. prices in all major categories. The exception was health care paid by individuals—Canadian prices increased by 120 per cent compared to a 162 per cent jump in the United States.

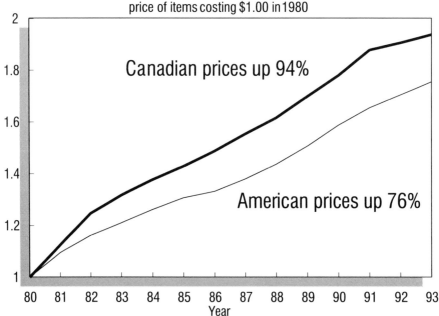

CONSUMER PRICES
price of items costing $1.00 in 1980

Sources: Statistics Canada, Catalogue 62-010. U.S. Bureau of the Census, Statistical Abstracts of the United States.

59/THE 1980s WERE STAGNANT FOR FAMILY INCOMES

Inflation has wiped out family income gains.

In 1980, the median family income in both Canada and the United States was about $26,000. By 1992, this median family income had risen to almost $48,000 in Canada and to $46,000 in the United States. The 1980 to 1992 increase was an "incredible" 85 per cent in Canada and 75 per cent in the United States. Sounds too good to be true? It is!

Inflation has been at work in both countries with Canada experiencing the greatest price increases over the period. When inflation is removed from the growth in actual incomes, the Canadian family experienced a real 4 per cent decline in median income over the decade, while the American family managed to move ahead by only 3 per cent. In real terms, families are still at virtually the same financial spot that they were when the 1980s began.

Additional taxation has caused further downward movement in family incomes in Canada and has turned the small gain in the United States into a negative.

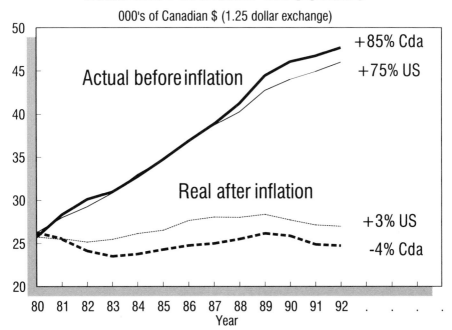

MEDIAN FAMILY INCOMES

000's of Canadian $ (1.25 dollar exchange)

Actual before inflation +85% Cda +75% US

Real after inflation +3% US -4% Cda

Year

Sources: Statistics Canada, Catalogue 13-207. U.S. Bureau of the Census, Current Population Report P60-180.

60/INDIVIDUALS STAY JUST AHEAD OF INFLATION

"Unattached" individuals in "non-family households" are people who either live alone or with persons to whom they are not related. Roughly one in every seven persons in both countries lives in this kind of household.

Non-family individuals in Canada have traditionally had lower incomes than the same group in the United States. This trend continued into 1992 with median annual incomes of just under $18,000 in Canada, and about $19,000 in the United States. It is reasonable to expect non-family individuals to earn much lower incomes than family households because, by definition, only one person is available for work.

Incomes of Canadian non-family individuals rose by 98 per cent from 1980 to 1992, while the American increase was 83 per cent. After removing the impact of higher inflation in Canada, non-family individual incomes increased by 4 per cent in Canada. In the United States, the real gain was a stronger 7 per cent. Taxation has reduced or reversed these gains in both countries.

MEDIAN INCOMES OF NON-FAMILY INDIVIDUALS

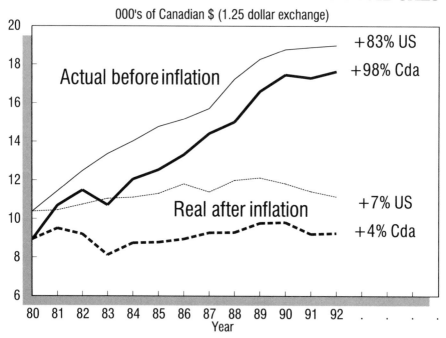

000's of Canadian $ (1.25 dollar exchange)

Actual before inflation

+83% US

+98% Cda

Real after inflation

+7% US

+4% Cda

Year

Sources: Statistics Canada, Catalogue 13-207. U.S. Bureau of the Census, Current Population Report P60-180.

61 /YES, CANADIANS DO PAY MORE TAXES

Canadians pay more taxes and complain more about that fact.

Gallup surveys conducted in 1993 found that 77 per cent of Canadians believe that their taxes are too high, compared to 55 per cent of Americans who think that way about their own taxes.

The Organization for Economic Co-operation and Development (OECD) has developed a compatible system for comparing taxes in different countries. The OECD has classified taxes collected on incomes of persons as a tax. They have also classified as a tax most "compulsory" social security contributions which are paid by employees and other persons. No tabulation is available to measure retail taxes and other taxes.

In 1991, total personal income taxes plus social security contributions averaged about $11,500 per household in Canada and about $10,500 in the United States. These taxes and contributions now represent about 27 per cent (as per OECD) of average household income in Canada and a much lower 22 per cent in the United States. Both taxes and contributions have risen faster in Canada.

PERSONAL INCOME AND SOCIAL SECURITY TAXES AVERAGE DOLLARS PER HOUSEHOLD
(Canadian dollars, 1.25 exchange)

		Canada		**United States**	
		1980	1991	1980	1991
		dollars		dollars	
Personal income taxes:	$	4,275	10,303	3,534	7,648
Social security contributions by employees, self-employed and not employed:	$	490	1,275	1,283	2,916
TOTAL:	$	4,765	11,578	4,817	10,564
Total as percentage of average household income:	$	20%	27%	17%	22%

Sources: Organization for Economic Co-operation and Development, Revenue Statistics of OECD Member Countries, 1965-1991. Gallup Canada, *The Gallup Report. The Gallup Monthly* (U.S.).

62/AMERICANS HAVE MORE DEBT OVERALL

The average Canadian and American owes a lot of money. Some of the money was borrowed by governments and the rest by citizens themselves.

For many years, governments have been spending more than they collect in taxes and other revenues. The shortfall is debt. In 1981, Canadian government debt at all levels was equal to $18,850 per household; by 1992 the debt load exceeded $57,000. Government debt per household also tripled in the United States to about $52,000 per household in 1992. Canadian governments have clearly accumulated more debt per household.

In contrast, Americans have to support more personal debt. Consumer credit and mortgage debt per household in the United States is about equal to the level of government debt, and it is over 25 per cent higher than the level of consumer and mortgage debt for Canadians.

Adding up what governments have borrowed, plus what households have borrowed themselves, leads to a surprising conclusion—the average American household is more indebted than the average Canadian household.

TOTAL GOVERNMENT AND HOUSEHOLD DEBT DOLLARS PER HOUSEHOLD
(Canadian dollars, 1.25 exchange)

	Canadians		Americans	
	1981	1992	1981	1992
Government debt:	$18,850	57,240	17,225	51,924
Consumer credit and mortgages:	$19,346	40,230	21,318	51,103
TOTAL DEBT:	$38,196	97,470	38,543	103,027

Source: Statistics Canada, National Balance Sheet Accounts, preliminary, uncatalogued. U.S. Flow of Funds Accounts, 4th Quarter 1992

63/WOMEN ARE NARROWING THE INCOME GAP

Women continue to earn less than men, even though women now hold 46 per cent of all jobs in both Canada and the United States.

A Canadian woman working at a full-time job for a full year in 1992 earned a median income of about $26,500, compared to $36,500 for a man in the same situation. The typical woman in Canada now earns about 73 per cent of what a man does. In the United States the ratio is 71 per cent.

As for relative improvement in women's income, Americans played catch-up during the early 1980s where the ratio increased from 60 per cent during the early 1980s to about 65 per cent during the middle of the decade. The Canadian ratio exceeded the American rate until the middle of the decade, and both have generally moved up together since then.

The relative income situation between women and men is closest among younger age groups and for those with higher levels of education in both countries. The gap will narrow further as females continue to move into occupations and senior positions traditionally held by males—the process is slow.

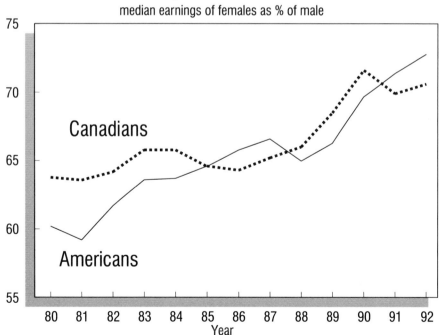

FEMALE TO MALE EARNINGS
FULL-TIME, FULL-YEAR WORKERS
median earnings of females as % of male

Sources: Statistics Canada, Catalogue 13-217. U.S. Bureau of the Census, Statistical Abstracts of the United States.

64/INCOME INEQUALITY IS GROWING AMONG AMERICANS

Equality of incomes is often stated as a goal of public policy. The theory goes that everyone should have the opportunity to benefit from the incomes created by the combined strength of the people of a nation. Others suggest that inequality encourages people to work harder to move into higher-income categories.

One of the easiest-to-understand measures of income inequality simply compares how much income the richest 20 per cent of households report in a year compared to the poorest 20 per cent of households. It is a measure used by the United Nations.

In 1980, the top 20 per cent of Canadian households had aggregate incomes 10 times larger than the poorest 20 per cent. The trend indicates a slight reduction in inequality with the ratio of the richest to the poorest in Canada down to 9.5 times in 1992.

The opposite is true among Americans where inequality worsened during the decade. By 1992, the richest 20 per cent of American households had aggregate incomes 12.3 times larger than the poorest 20 per cent.

HOUSEHOLD INCOME INEQUALITY

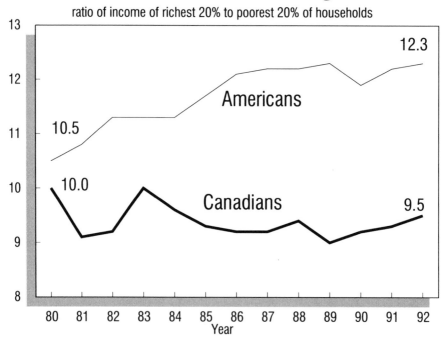

ratio of income of richest 20% to poorest 20% of households

Sources: Statistics Canada, Catalogue 13-207. U.S. Bureau of the Census, Current Population Report P60-180.

65/THE RICH GET AN EVEN BIGGER PIECE OF THE PIE

The rich are getting an even bigger piece of the pie!

Who is rich? Who is poor? Who is in the middle? A simple and insightful way to form "income compatible groups" is to line up all households from the poorest to the richest in terms of annual incomes. The 40 per cent at the bottom are the poorest, the next 40 percent are the middle, and the top 20 per cent are the richest.

The top 20 per cent of households in Canada took in 42.1 per cent of all Canadian incomes reported in 1980. By 1992, their share had risen to 43.6 per cent. In the United States, the richest group increased their share even faster, moving up to 46.9 per cent from 44 per cent in 1980.

Over the period, the Canadian high-income group gained about 1.5 percentage points of income while the middle income group lost the same amount. In the United States, the 2.9 percentage point gain by the richest group came at the expense of both the middle class and the poorest class.

SHARE OF TOTAL HOUSEHOLD INCOMES BEFORE TAX

	Canadians		**Americans**	
	1980/1992	Gain/ loss	1980/1992	Gain/ loss
	% of total incomes		**% of total incomes**	
Richest 20% of households:	42.1/43.6	+1.5	44.0/46.9	+2.9
Middle 40% of households:	43.0/41.5	−1.5	41.6/40.0	-1.6
Poorest 40% of households:	14.9/14.9	—	14.4/13.2	-1.2

Sources: Statistics Canada, Catalogue 13-207. U.S. Bureau of the Census, Current Population Report P60-180.

66/WEALTH NOT EQUALLY DISTRIBUTED

Sell all your assets and pay off all your debts—what you have left is your wealth, or what some people like to call "net worth."

It is very difficult to collect accurate data on wealth, and few attempts have been made. Fortunately, both countries developed wealth estimates for 1984. Those studies found that median wealth per household was about $40,000 in both countries.

The distribution of total wealth is far from equal. The richest 20 per cent of households had accumulated about 45 per cent of the wealth in Canada. In the United States, this top group had a share closer to 48 per cent. In both countries the share of wealth held by the richest 20 percent was just a bit greater than the share (percentage) of annual incomes earned. (See previous page.)

The middle 40 per cent of households had 37 per cent of the wealth in Canada, compared to 33 per cent in the United States. The bottom 40 per cent had only 19 per cent of the wealth in either country.

SHARE OF TOTAL WEALTH (NET WORTH) 1984

	Canadians*	Americans
	% of total wealth	
Richest 20% of households:	45	48
Middle 40% of households:	37	33
Poorest 40% of households:	19	19

Does not add up to 100 due to rounding.

Sources: Statistics Canada, Catalogue 13-580. U.S. Bureau of the Census, Current Population Reports, P70-22.

67/POVERTY IS MUCH HIGHER IN AMERICA

The debate on how to measure poverty continues. By any definition, significant poverty exists in Canada, but it is especially evident in the United States.

T.M. Smeeding has done extensive research comparing international poverty rates during the 1980s. He defines poverty as family incomes 40 per cent or less of the median income in the relevant country, adjusted for family size.

Without government cash transfers, about 17 per cent of all Canadians would be living in poverty compared to about 20 per cent of Americans. Government cash transfers include such items as family allowance, food stamps, social assistance and other transfers. After taxes and government cash transfers, the Canadian poverty rate is reduced to 7 per cent, and the American rate falls to about 13 per cent. The American system for income redistribution is far less effective in reducing overall poverty rates.

The poverty rate after taxes and government transfers for children is estimated at about 9 per cent in Canada. In the United States, about one of every five children lives in poverty, even when measurements are adjusted to an after-tax and after-government cash transfer basis.

POVERTY RATES – MID 1980s

	Canada	United States
	(without taxes and government cash transfers)	
All persons:	17%	20%
Children (newborn to age 17):	16%	22%
	(with taxes and government cash transfers)	
All persons:	7%	13%
Children (newborn to age 17):	9%	20%

Sources: T.M. Smeeding from tables in Economic Policy Institute, *The State of Working America.* Armonk, N.Y.: M.E Sharpe, Inc., 1993.

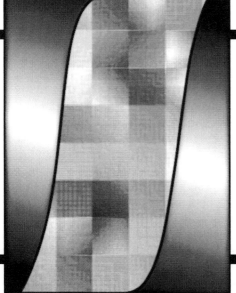

*HAPPINESS,
GOOD
HEALTH
AND
SAFETY*

SEARCHING FOR THE GOOD LIFE

"The good life" contains elements of material comforts, physical, spiritual and mental health, and safety. The vast majority of Canadians and Americans are very happy with life as it is right now.

Canadians and Americans seem to be living at similar levels relative to material comforts, even if they are more equally distributed in Canada.

Major differences are evident relative to health care. Canada is definitely a "kinder and gentler nation" in this respect, and Canadians are proud of the difference. The people of Saskatchewan, where Canada's health care system was first created, are especially proud. I am proud to live there.

How can the inequitable American health system have persisted for so long? Virtually everybody in the United States believes that the Canadian system (or the British model) is better, and that the American system needs to be rebuilt or greatly altered. The cheaper and more effective Canadian system is a winner for both individuals and companies. We should hope that Americans will have the courage to move beyond the interest of pressure groups and take forceful action to ensure better access to health care for all its citizens. The Canadian system did not come easy and it too must adapt and change.

What is happening on the safety side of the good life? American media thrive on news stories about violent crime. The picture we get is one in which the United States seems to be overrun with violent crime, while Canada is more peaceful. This perception (and the reality) is true for murders. The reality is less true for other crimes.

I was very surprised to discover that the percentage of households who respond that they are touched by crime is the same in both Canada and the United States. I was even more surprised—actually incredulous—to uncover in the official statistics that the rate of property and violent crime actually reported to police is *higher* in Canada than in the United States. Canada either has more crime than we think, or we are just more prone to report it. Part of the difference is due to definitional problems. Even so, the number of reported violent crimes is definitely rising much faster in Canada. Perhaps Canada's higher unemployment rate may help to explain the rapidly increasing violent Canadian crime rates.

Would the murder rate be higher in Canada if handguns were more easily available? I believe so. In the United States, people seem to shoot each other, while in Canada we either resort to fisticuffs or call the police to help us solve our disputes. I favour the Canadian way.

68/AMERICANS EAT OUT A LOT MORE

Money in, money out—this helps keeps the economy moving! The allocation of incomes varies substantially in each country.

A compatible survey of household spending is available for 1986. (Two 1990 surveys are available but are not compatible and, therefore, are not used here.) Canadians disburse about 14 per cent of total household incomes on food compared to 13 per cent for Americans. More significantly, Americans spend about 42 per cent of their food budget away from home in contrast to just 25 per cent among Canadians.

Compared to Americans, Canadians allocate significantly less of total incomes to housing, transportation and health care. One of the greatest absolute differences is the allocation for health care: Canadians earmark 1.8 percent of total household incomes on health compared to 4.6 percent for American households. Americans spend much less on tobacco and alcohol by percentage given the much lower prices for these items in the United States.

In 1986, personal income taxes absorbed almost 19 per cent of Canadian household incomes, more than double the U.S. income tax burden.

DISPOSITION OF HOUSEHOLD INCOMES – 1986

	Canadians	Americans
	% distribution of total incomes	
Food:	13.9	13.2
- at home	10.5	7.6
- away from home	3.4	5.6
Housing:	23.5	27.9
Transportation:	12.9	18.5
Clothing/apparel:	6.1	5.1
Entertainment:	5.0	4.5
Personal care:	1.9	1.1
Health care:	1.8	4.3
Education/reading:	1.4	1.8
Tobacco/alcohol:	3.2	2.0
Other: insurance, security, pensions, savings	11.5	12.9
Personal income taxes:	18.8	8.7
TOTAL	100.0	100.0

Sources: Statistics Canada, *Perspectives,* Autumn 1990, and Catalogue 62-555.U.S. Bureau of the Census, Statistical Abstracts of the United States.

69/BIG-TICKET ITEMS ARE FOUND IN MOST HOUSEHOLDS

Home conveniences and entertainment items are widely found in modern households.

Canadian and American households display many similar ownership patterns. Roughly two out of every three homes are owned by the people who live in them, and 83 to 89 per cent have one or more motor vehicles parked in the driveway. Telephones and colour televisions are found in most homes in both countries. Three-quarters of all homes now have VCRs, and the ratio is rising rapidly. Microwave oven ownership is also increasing in both countries.

Approximately three-quarters of homes have automatic clothes washers, but Canadians are more likely to have dryers.

Two items show sharply different ownership rates. Air-conditioning is found in about one-quarter of Canadian homes compared to 70 per cent of homes in the United States. The situation is the reverse relative to the ownership of freezers. Some cool information!

PERCENTAGE OF HOUSEHOLDS POSSESSING VARIOUS ITEMS (early 1990s)

	Canadians	Americans
Colour television:	98%	96%
Telephone:	98%	94%
Motor vehicle:	83%	89%
Microwave oven:	76%	79%
Clothes washer:	75%	76%
Clothes dryer:	74%	69%
VCR:	74%	72%
Own home:	63%	64%
Freezer:	58%	35%
Automatic dishwasher:	44%	43%
Air-conditioning:	27%	70%

Sources: Statistics Canada, Catalogue, 64-202. U.S. Bureau of the Census, Statistical Abstracts of the United States.

70/NET WORTH IS ALMOST IDENTICAL

The good life is usually associated with an accumulation of wealth.

Compatible wealth estimates are available for the mid-1980s. At that time, the median wealth or net worth was about $40,000 per household in both Canada and the United States. At the "median wealth" level, half of all households have more wealth and half have less.

As a group, young households have little wealth and pull down the median value. Median wealth rises until the age of 55 to 64, peaking at $83,000 in Canada and $91,000 in the United States. America's elderly are significantly wealthier than are those in Canada. Husband-wife families hold about $60,000 of net worth in both countries.

Equity in a home is the single-most important form of wealth accumulation. This is clearly evident in the fact that home owners have accumulated about $80,000 of wealth in both countries, compared to only a few thousand dollars for renters. Financial assets comprise about 20 per cent of the wealth in each country.

MEDIAN NET WORTH (WEALTH) - ALL HOUSEHOLDS -1984
(Canadian dollars – 1.25 exchange)

	Canadians	**Americans**
All households:	$39,900	$40,300
By age of head of household:		
under 35	not much	not much
35-44	$46,400	$43,900
45-54	$75,800	$72,600
55-64	$82,600	$91,000
65+	$55,600	$74,400
Husband-wife families:	$58,000	$61,900
Home owners:	$80,000	$78,100
Renters:	$3,300	$2,400
Per cent of net worth due to equity in home:	34%	41%

Sources: Statistics Canada, Catalogue 13-580. U.S. Bureau of the Census, Current Population Reports, P70-22.

71/VISITING ACROSS THE BORDERLINE

Canadians are much more likely to visit the United States than is the case in reverse.

The majority of all travel between each country is of short duration. In 1993, about three-quarters of all Canadian visits to the United States were same-day (that is, return the same day) trips with about two-thirds of American visits to Canada being same-day trips. In that year, Canadians made almost 50 million same-day trips to the United States, while Americans made about 21 million same-day trips to Canada.

Canadians also take more trips of longer duration. In 1992, Canadians made some 18.6 million person-trips of at least one night to the United States, with an opposite flow at just under 12 million. The average stay for such longer trips is 7.4 days for Canadian visitors and 3.9 days for American visitors. The average Canadian spends $426 (Canadian) per trip to the United States, while Americans spend $312 (Canadian) per trip.

CHARACTERISTICS OF TRAVELLERS STAYING ONE OR MORE NIGHTS – 1992

	Canadians visiting United States	Americans visiting Canada
Total person-trips:	18.6 million	11.8 million
Average number of nights:	7.4	3.9
Per cent of person-trips by car:	73%	70%
Per cent of person-trips by purpose:		
-business	12%	15%
-visiting friends	16%	19%
-pleasure/other	72%	66%
Top destinations:	New England (25%) Pacific (16%) East-North Central (13%)	Ontario (49%) B.C. (21%) Quebec (14%)
Total spending(C$):	$7.9 billion	$3.7 billion
Spending per person-trip(C$):	$426	$312
Spending per person-night(C$):	$58	$80

Source: Statistics Canada, Catalogue 66-201.

72/HEALTH CARE IS CHEAPER AND BETTER IN CANADA

Spend less but get more. This is the reality for Canadian health.

Canada spends about 9 per cent of its Gross Domestic Product (GDP) on health care compared to over 12 per cent in the United States. The $2,100 spent per year on the average Canadian is 30 per cent less than in the United States.

The number of persons per doctor is similar in both countries, but the number of persons per nurse is 23 per cent higher in the United States.

The average Canadian spends 1.5 days per year in a hospital compared to 0.9 day for the average American. More frequent use of hospitals in Canada translates to a higher average occupancy rate. An occupied bed in Canada is supported by 3.3 full-time (or equivalent) employees compared to 5.5 in the United States.

Canadians have a more effective system insofar as longer life expectancy—when calculated both at birth and at age 65. And, the Canadian mortality rate for young children is 40 per cent below the American rate.

HEALTH SERVICE HEALTH STATUS INDICATORS

1990
HEALTH SERVICE

	Canada	United States
Health expenditures as a percentage of GDP:	9.2%	12.4%
Health expenditures per person (C$ at 1990 exchange rate):	$2,147	$3,025
Population per doctor:	448	434
Population per nurse:	120	147
Patient days per person per year:	1.5	.9
Hospital occupancy rate:	79%	67%
Full-time equivalent employees per occupied hospital bed:	3.3	5.5

HEALTH STATUS

Life expectancy at birth:	77	75.9
Life expectancy at age 65:		
-male	15.3	15.0
-female	19.8	18.9
Under age 5 mortality rate per 1,000 live births:	8	13

Source: Statistics Canada, Catalogue 82-003.

73/AMERICANS PREFER CANADIAN HEALTH SYSTEM

Americans do not like their health care system.

A 1992 Gallup Report found that Canadians are much happier with their health care system than are Americans. Over 70 per cent of Canadians rate local health care as "excellent" or "good" compared to under 60 per cent among Americans. Americans clearly believe that the costs of their system are very high.

Canadians overwhelmingly prefer their own system, whereas only one-quarter of Americans believe they have the better system. Virtually no Canadian wants an American-style system.

An older Harris/Harvard survey had found that about 56 per cent of Canadian adults believe that their health-care system works pretty well and that only minor changes are necessary to make it better. Only 10 per cent of Americans feel the same way, and almost 30 per cent believe their system is so bad that it has to be completely rebuilt.

About 8 per cent of Americans claim they are not getting needed medical care for financial reasons—over one-third of these people are uninsured.

SATISFACTION WITH HEALTH CARE

	Canadians	Americans
Percentage who rate local health care as excellent/good:	71% ('92)	59% ('92)
Percentage who believe costs are very high:	19% ('92)	57% ('92)
Percentage who believe own country has a better system of health care:	91% ('92)	26% ('92)
Percentage who believe that the other country has a better system of health care:	3% ('92)	43% ('92)
Percentage who believe health-care system works pretty well and only minor changes are necessary to make it better:	56% ('88)	10% ('88)

Percentage who believe that
the system is so bad that
it has to be completely rebuilt: 5% ('88)   29% ('88)

Percentage who are not
receiving needed medical care
for financial reasons: 1% ('88)   8% ('88)

Sources: R.J. Blendon and H. Taylor in Health Affairs, Spring 1989. *The Gallup Monthly Report* (U.S.).

74/NOT SURE THAT MORE AMERICANS ARE TOUCHED BY CRIME

Some crimes are reported to police, but many are not. For this reason, occasional surveys of households are conducted wherein respondents are asked more directly whether they have been touched by crime.

A 1993 Statistics Canada survey reported that 24 per cent of Canadian households had been directly affected by crime. A similar survey, conducted in 1991 by the United States Bureau of Justice Statistics, found that an identical 24 per cent of American households had been touched by crime. Urban crime is much more prevalent than rural crime in both countries. Fewer Canadians claim they are afraid to walk alone in their communities at night.

A 1989 Decima/*Maclean's* survey revealed that 21 per cent of Canadians and 26 per cent of Americans said they had been "robbed or assaulted." Only 3 per cent of Canadians own a handgun compared to 24 per cent of Americans, but a large majority in both countries want more restrictive gun control. About the same percentage of Canadians and Americans admit they have used illegal drugs.

CRIME AS MEASURED BY HOUSEHOLD SURVEYS

		Canadians	Americans
Percentage of households	-Total:	24% ('93)	24% ('91)
who say they are	-Urban	27% ('93)	29% ('91)
touched by crime:	-Rural	17% ('93)	17% ('91)
Percentage who say they have been robbed or assaulted:		21% ('89)	26% ('89)
Percentage who fear walking alone on the streets of their community at night:		35% ('93)	44% ('92)
Percentage who own a handgun:		3% ('89)	24% ('89)
Percentage who favour more restrictive gun control laws:		77% ('94)	70% ('93)
Percentage who say they have used illegal drugs:		11% ('89)	13% ('89)

Sources: Statistics Canada, Catalogue 85-002. U.S. Bureau of the Census, *Statistical Abstracts of the United States. Maclean's*, "Portrait of Two Nations", July 3, 1989. Gallup Canada, *The Gallup Report. The Gallup Poll Monthly* (U.S.).

75/VIOLENT CRIME IS RISING FASTER IN CANADA

Canadians assume that total crime rates are much higher in the United States. This is not evident from the official police numbers.

Police classify reported crimes into two major categories—"property" and "violent". About 90 per cent of reported crime in both countries is property crime. Official published numbers lead to the following conclusion: Canada has a higher level of reported crime for both categories. This is so even though Americans have rates several times higher for selected crimes, such as murder and violent sexual assault. Definitional problems (common assault, which accounts for 60 per cent of violent crime in Canada, is excluded from the U.S. violent category) and the apparent lower frequency of crime reporting in the United States combine to produce a conclusion which seems opposite to the typical perception of reality. Household surveys do, however, indicate similar rates of crime in the United States (see "Not Sure that More Americans Are Touched by Crime").

Two conclusions are clear. The growth in the rate of reported crime in the "violent" category is rising much faster in Canada. Property crime has been relatively flat in both countries.

"REPORTED" CRIME TRENDS
rate of crimes reported now for every 100 reported in 1980

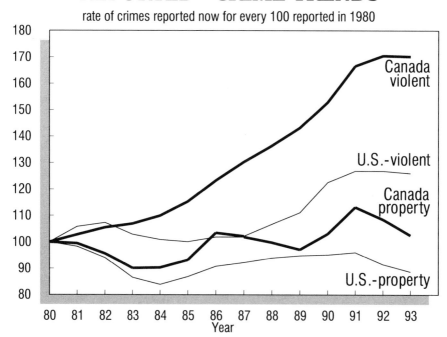

Sources: Statistics Canada, Catalogue 85-002. U.S. Bureau of the Census, Statistical Abstracts of the United States.

76 /HAPPIER CANADIANS WORRY MORE ABOUT THE FUTURE

Pollster Angus Reid carried out a survey in 16 countries to compare and contrast Canadians in an international perspective. The results were published in 1992 in *Canada and the World.*

The study found that Canadians are a happy lot, ranking third in terms of happiness "with life as it is right now." Americans are close behind percentage-wise (86 per cent vs. 82 per cent), though they rank ninth of 16.

Both Canadians and Americans feel they now have a high degree of freedom to say what they want about their governments. Canadians are more likely to say that it is a real struggle to get by financially.

Canadians and Americans are generally optimistic about the future. Canadians seem to be a bit less optimistic regarding our future quality of life and about whether our children will fare as well as we have. Canadians, however, worry much less about our financial ability to survive major surgery.

HAPPINESS – NOW AND IN THE FUTURE – 1992

	Canadians	Americans
Percentage who agree that they are very happy with life as it is right now:	86%	82%
Percentage who agree that they have the personal freedom to say anything about the government:	88%	87%
Percentage who agree that it is a real struggle just to get by financially:	60%	55%
Percentage who are optimistic about the prospects for their personal quality of life during the next decade:	69%	74%
Percentage who think that their children will be better off than they are:	35%	41%
Percentage who would worry about paying for surgery for a family member:	26%	41%

Source: Angus Reid, *Canada and the World: An International Perspective on Canada and Canadians,* 1992.

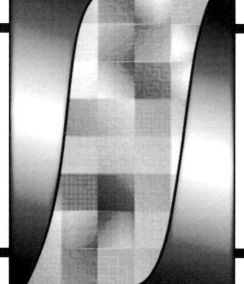

*BEYOND
THE
AVERAGES*

A LOOK AT
SPECIAL GROUPS

When I began to research this book, it became very clear that Canadians and Americans are not homogeneous within their own countries. The short write-ups on individual topics could not incorporate more than a few of these differences within each country. To partially compensate for this short-coming, I have prepared short overviews on four special groups, plus I have examined some regional differences.

I am struck especially by the dire situation in which many Black Americans are living; as a group, they are statistically characterized by significantly less education, double the U.S. rate of unemployment, over triple the poverty rate, much lower average incomes, and virtually no wealth accumulation. The group's social fabric is unsettling—two-thirds of Black children are born to unwed mothers. The situation for Hispanic Americans is similar on the economic front, but more stable on the social side.

The economic situation seems to be better for Black Canadians, at least relative to incomes. Incomes are 85 per cent of the overall Canadian average. This stands in contrast to under 60 per cent for Black Americans.

The statistics on Aboriginal Canadians are also very disturbing. It is difficult to be overly proud of a country that allows the extremes to continue to exist. Recent "horror" stories, including high suicide rates, portray terrible conditions on many reserves in Canada. More must be done to foster healthier Aboriginal communities in Canada—the Indian Act has not worked. Conditions among native American Indians in the United States seem to be just a bit better than in Canada; the unemployment rate for Indians is "only" double the U.S. national average.

I have highlighted Quebec because of its special and distinctive place in Canada. The selected indicators suggest that Quebec lags behind the averages for the whole of Canada in economic terms, but that these differences are rather small. The province's social fabric is definitely more open. Quebec has been able to sustain French as its dominant language. This fact and other characteristics make it a distinct place from the rest of Canada. Quebecers have their own heroes.

Canadians and Quebecers must find a way to maintain and foster the uniqueness of Quebec within Canada. The differences between Quebec and the rest of Canada are real, and the general acceptance of this reality helps define the Canada in which I want to live. My Canada includes Quebec and French-speaking Canadians like myself, throughout Canada. It also includes English-speaking persons in Quebec. I want my government to offer services in both French and English, to people in all parts of Canada.

77/ "EN FRANCAIS" AND MORE DIFFERENCES FOR QUEBEC

Over 80 per cent of Quebecois speak French. French is spoken in 23 per cent of all Canadian households.

Almost everyone who lives in Chicoutimi, Trois-Rivières, and Quebec City speak French at home most of the time. Approximately 70 per cent of the people of Montreal, Canada's second-largest metropolitan area, speak French at home. Outside of Quebec, Ottawa has the largest share of Canadians who speak French, at 30 per cent.

The median age of Quebecers is almost identical with the median age of all Canadians—34 years. Compared to all of Canada, Quebecers achieve about the same level of education; they are somewhat less likely to be in the labour force and are a bit more likely to be unemployed. Median family incomes, and especially net worth, are lower in Quebec. Poverty is the plight of 16 per cent of Quebec families, compared to 13 per cent for all of Canada. Quebecers are more likely to be renters.

Quebecers have fewer traditional families, with a smaller percentage of married couples and more births to unmarried mothers. Quebecers tend to have slightly smaller families.

QUEBECOIS SELECTED SOCIAL AND ECONOMIC CHARACTERISTICS*
(mostly early 1990s - bracketed numbers are for all of Canada)

Population	**6,895,960**	
Percentage with French as the home language:	83%	(23%)
Highest percentage of French as the home language in metropolitan areas:	99% Chicoutimi 99% Trois-Rivières 98% Quebec City	
Median age:	**34.2**	**(33.5)**
Percentage who have a university degree (age 25+):	12%	(13%)
Percentage of age 15 and over in labour force:	63%	(66%)
Percentage unemployed:	13%	(11%)
Median income of families:	$42,700	($46,700)
Percentage of families who are below the poverty level:	16%	(13%)

Median household net worth:	$29,500	($39,900)
Percentage who own homes:	56%	(63%)
Percentage of families with married couples:	69%	(77%)
Percentage of births to unmarried mothers:	30%	(24%)
Percentage of children to married couples:	67%	(74%)
Persons per family:	3.0	(3.1)

* Canadian definitions and dollars.

Sources: Statistics Canada, Catalogue 13-207, 13-580, 82-553, 93-310, 93-311, 93-312, 93-317, 93-328.

78/HARDSHIP IS COMMON FOR MANY BLACK AMERICANS

Black Americans do not have it easy!

Black Americans number about 32 million in the United States, comprising almost 12 per cent of the total population. Projections anticipate the Black American population to reach 38 million by 2005.

The highest concentrations of black people within metropolitan areas are in Jackson, Memphis and Montgomery (43, 41 and 36 per cent respectively). The median age of Black Americans is 28 years, compared to over 34 years for White Americans.

Compared to White Americans, Black Americans achieve less education; fewer are in the labour force and they are twice as likely to be unemployed. On the income side, Black American families earn incomes which average less than 60 per cent of white families; they are almost four times more likely to live below the poverty level, and their household net worth is only one-tenth of what it is for white U.S. households.

Half of Black American families are comprised of a married couple; almost two-thirds of births are to single mothers; only one-third of children live with two parents. Black American families tend to be larger than the average U.S. family.

BLACK AMERICANS
SELECTED SOCIAL AND ECONOMIC CHARACTERISTICS*
(mostly early 1990s - bracketed numbers are for U.S. white population)

Population	**31,895,000**	
highest percentage of population in metropolitan areas:	43% — Jackson, Mississippi 41% — Memphis, Tennessee 36% — Montgomery, Alabama	
Median age	**28.1**	**(34.4)**
Percentage with 4 or more years of college (age 25+):	12%	(22%)
Percentage of age 16 and over in labour force:	63%	(67%)
Percentage unemployed:	12%	(6%)
Median income of families(US$):	$21,400	($36,900)
Percentage of families below the poverty level:	29%	(8%)
Median household net worth(US$):	$4,200	($43,300)

Percentage who own homes:	43%	(67%)
Percentage who voted in 1992 election:	54%	(64%)
Percentage of families comprised of a married couple:	49%	(83%)
Percentage of births to unmarried mothers:	65%	(19%)
Percentage of children living with both parents:	36%	(79%)
Persons per family:	3.5	(3.1)

* United States definitions and dollars.

Sources: U.S. Bureau of the Census, Statistical Abstracts of the United States.

79/HISPANIC AMERICANS ARE ONE STEP AHEAD OF BLACK AMERICANS

Hispanic Americans seem to be marginally better off than Black Americans.

Official sources indicate that 22 million Hispanic people call the United States home, with 34 million projected to live in the U.S. by the year 2005. The three Texas metropolitan centres of Laredo, McAllen, and El Paso have very high concentrations of Hispanics.

The median age of Hispanic Americans is nine years younger than for White Americans.

In comparison to White Americans, Hispanic Americans achieve less education; they are just as likely to be in the workforce, but they experience more unemployment. Median family incomes for Hispanics are 63 per cent of the incomes of white U.S. families, and one-quarter of Hispanic families live in poverty. Net worth per household is only $5,500 compared to $43,300 for White Americans. About four in 10 own their homes. Hispanics are better off than Black Americans for five of these seven indicators.

Only 29 per cent of Hispanics voted during the 1992 U.S. federal election.

Hispanic family structures and relationships average somewhere between the situation for White and Black Americans. Hispanic Americans have the highest number of persons per family of the three comparison groups.

HISPANIC AMERICANS
SELECTED SOCIAL AND ECONOMIC CHARACTERISTICS*
(mostly early 1990s - bracketed numbers are for U.S. white population)

Population	**22,354,000**	
Highest percentage of metropolitan areas:	94% — Laredo, Texas	
	85% — McAllen, Texas	
	70% — El Paso, Texas	
Median age:	**25.5**	**(34.4)**
Percentage with 4 or more years of college (age 25+):	10%	(22%)
Percentage of age 16 and over in labour force:	66%	(67%)
Percentage unemployed:	10%	(6%)
Median income of families (US$):	$23,400	($36,900)

Percentage of families		
below poverty level:	25%	(8%)
Median household net worth (US$):	$5,500	($43,300)
Percentage who own homes:	39%	(67%)

Percentage who voted in		
1992 election:	29%	(64%)

Percentage of families		
comprised of a married couple:	69%	(83%)
Percentage of births to		
unmarried mothers:	36%	(19%)
Percentage of children living		
with both parents:	66%	(79%)
Persons per family:	3.9	(3.1)

* United States definitions and dollars.

Sources: U.S. Bureau of the Census, Statistical Abstracts of the United States.

80/THE STRUGGLE FOR CANADIAN ABORIGINALS

The number of Aboriginal people in Canada is estimated to be as high as one million and growing faster than the total population. North American Indians comprise 46 per cent of the Canadian Aboriginal population with the remainder being self-identified as Métis. Aboriginals as a group are much younger compared to the average Canadian.

More then 2,200 reserves cover an area equal to about half the size of Nova Scotia.

Aboriginals are clearly lagging behind the economic and social situation of other Canadians. Average incomes are only 70 per cent of the Canadian average, with over half of Aboriginal adults earning an annual income under $10,000. Participation in the labour force is lowest for Indians on reserves with unemployment on reserves almost triple the national average. Conditions are somewhat better for Aboriginal people living off reserves, and for the Métis.

Life expectancy among North American Indians is about eight years shorter than for all Canadians, but the gap seems to be getting smaller. Youth mortality and suicide rates are very high.

ABORIGINAL CANADIANS
SELECTED SOCIAL AND ECONOMIC CHARACTERISTICS*
(1991 unless indicated - bracketed numbers are for all Canada)

Population	**625,710 to 1,002,675**	
highest percentage of metropolitan areas:	6% — Saskatoon, Sask.	
	6% — Regina, Sask.	
	5% — Winnipeg, Man.	
Percentage of population under age 25:	57%	(35%)
Percentage with post-secondary education (ages 15-49):	33%	(51%)
Percentage of ages 15 and over in labour force:		
- Total	57%	(68%)
- North American Indian	55%	
- on reserve	45%	
- off reserve	61%	
- Métis	63%	

Percentage unemployed:

- Total	25%	(11%)
- North American Indian	26%	
- on reserve	31%	
- off reserve	23%	
- Métis	22%	
Average income (age 15+) (in 1985):	$12,899	($18,188)
Percentage of individuals with an income under $10,000:	54%	(34%)

* Canadian definitions and dollars.

Sources: Statistics Canada, Census of Canada, and Aboriginal Peoples Survey.

81 /EXTREMES BETWEEN STATES AND PROVINCES

The United States claims the three "best off" and the three "worst off" among states and provinces.

The best-off households are found in the state of Connecticut, with median household incomes of about $53,000, followed closely by New Jersey and Alaska. A total of 10 states have higher median household incomes than the best-off province in Canada; Ontario has the highest household income (close to $41,000) with British Columbia second and Alberta third.

The lowest median household incomes are found in Mississippi, West Virginia and Arkansas. Prince Edward Island is the worst off in Canada, but actually ranks ahead of the three poorest American states. Manitoba and Saskatchewan join the Canadian low-income group.

Family poverty rates, using unadjusted data, in the best-off states are generally half the rates found in the best-off provinces. In contrast, the poverty rates in the poorest states are generally higher than in Canada.

Surprise! Prince Edward Island has both the lowest incomes and the lowest poverty rates in Canada.

BEST-OFF AND WORST-OFF PROVINCES AND STATES

	Canada	United States
	Household Median Incomes	
	1991	1991
Highest	($35-41,000)	($50-53,000)
	Ontario	Connecticut
	British Columbia	New Jersey
	Alberta	Alaska
Lowest	($29-32,000)	($24-30,000)
	Prince Edward Is.	Mississippi
	Manitoba	West Virginia
	Saskatchewan	Arkansas
	Family Poverty Rates*	
	1991	1989
Lowest	(10-11%)	(4-6%)
	Prince Edward Is.	New Hampshire
	Ontario	Connecticut
	British Columbia	New Jersey

Highest	(16-17%)	(16-20%)
	Manitoba	Mississippi
	Newfoundland	Louisiana
	Quebec	New Mexico

* National definitions of poverty (i.e., not compatible). C$ at 1.25 exchange.

Sources: Statistics Canada, Catalogue 13-207. U.S. Bureau of the Census, Current Population Report P60-180, and 1990 Census of Population, CPH-5-1.

*ON
THE
WORLD
STAGE*

NO CLEAR WINNER IN WORLD RANKINGS

It is not easy to compare and summarize economic and human progress on a country-to-country basis. Even so, at least three groups have compiled comprehensive country rankings.

The good news! Canada ranks number one in the United Nations Human Development Index (1994). The United Nations believes that Canada is a very good place to live. Canada just beat out the United States when measured by the Where-We-Stand Index (1992).

Japan is the winner within one of the rankings. Japan has linked a sound educational system, hard work, a healthy population, high savings, effective business and government partnerships, and some restrictive trade policies into a winning combination in world markets. On the negative side, Japan has been less successful in fostering equality between men and women and in building individual freedom.

Canada may not be able to sustain its high ranking as a good place to live unless it can reverse its weakening competitive position. According to the 1994 World Economic Forum, Canadian competitiveness has slipped from fourth to 16th over the last few years. In contrast, the United States has moved up to number one on the competitiveness scale.

How can Canada improve its competitiveness? We must reduce trade barriers between provinces. Canada may have freer trade with the United States than it has between individual provinces. In addition, we must become more focused on supporting winning sectors such as communication and transportation services aimed at international markets rather than pouring money into dying or uncompetitive industries. Canadian governments and business must work together even more to gain markets; it works in Japan and Europe. Labour mobility must be promoted by the unemployment insurance system rather than be discouraged by it. Businesses must be encouraged to provide more and better internal training and development that fits the needs of their activities. Canada's very expensive educational system must become more sensitive to business needs by being more adaptable to changing markets and management practices and thinking.

Lastly, Canada must never again allow its interest rates to rise significantly above American rates for any extended length of time to support an overvalued dollar.

82/CANADA, U.S. AND JAPAN TOP WORLD RANKINGS

International research teams rank Canada, the United States and Japan high among the nations of the world.

The United Nations has developed a Human Development Index to summarize life expectancy, educational attainment and incomes. The selected dimensions reflect a "process of enlarging people's choices." Canada ranked first in the latest index, up from second spot the previous year. The United States ranked eighth, down from sixth a year earlier. In 1970, Canada also ranked first while the United States was a close second.

Michael Wolff and a large team of researchers published a book called *Where We Stand*. The study ranked countries according to seven groupings of activities. The addition (my summation) of the seven areas produced an overall index. Canada and the United States ranked fifth and sixth respectively. Japan was number one.

The World Economic Forum produces a scoreboard which ranks countries on their ability to compete. In this ranking, the United States ranks number one with Canada in 16th place.

SUMMARY OF TOP DOZEN OR SO IN WORLD RANKINGS

UNITED NATIONS HUMAN DEVELOPMENT INDEX - 1994	WHERE WE STAND SUMMARY INDEX - 1992	WORLD ECONOMIC COMPETITIVENESS SCOREBOARD - 1994
1. Canada	Japan	United States
2. Switzerland	Germany	Singapore
3. Japan	Sweden	Japan
4. Sweden	Switzerland	Hong Kong
5. Norway	Canada	Germany
6. France	United States	Switzerland
7. Australia	United Kingdom	Denmark
8. United States	Netherlands	Netherlands
9. Netherlands	Finland	New Zealand
10. United Kingdom	Norway	Sweden
11. Germany	Australia	Norway
12. Austria	France	Austria
16		Canada

Sources: United Nations Development Program, *Human Development Report 1993* and *1994*. Toronto: Oxford University Press. Michael Wolff, *Where We Stand*. New York: Bantam Books, 1992. World Economic Forum, *The World Competitiveness Report 1994*, Geneva.

83/TWO NATIONS IN AMERICA?

The United Nations found large human development disparities among Americans.

The latest United Nations Human Development Index ranks Canada as most advanced in terms of aggregate measures of life expectancy, educational attainment and per capita incomes. The United States ranks eighth. The previous report suggested that the United States may be one country, but two nations—White Americans and the rest. White Americans ranked in the top spot in the world while Black Americans ranked 31st, in line with Trinidad and Tobago; Hispanic Americans ranked in 35th spot, next to Estonia.

When the official index is adjusted for income distribution, Canada dips to eighth and the United States to 11th. With adjustments for gender equality, Canada dips to ninth spot and the United States falls to 12th position.

Canada and the United States receive high rankings in terms of the percentage of administrative and management jobs which are held by women.

UNITED NATIONS HUMAN DEVELOPMENT INDEX RANKINGS FOR COMPONENTS AND ALTERNATIVE MEASURES

HUMAN DEVELOPMENT INDEX

	Canada	United States	BEST
Total:	1	8	Canada
-adjusted for income distribution	8	11	Japan
-adjusted for gender disparity	9	12	Sweden

United Nations Rankings for Women

	Canada	United States	BEST
Life expectancy at birth:	6	14	Japan
Maternal mortality per live birth:	12	19	Iceland, Luxembourg
Percentage of women in administrative/management:	3	1	U.S.
Percentage of women in Parliament:	12	17	Finland

Sources: United Nations Development Program, *Human Development Report 1993* and *1994.* Toronto: Oxford University Press.

84/CANADIANS AND AMERICANS "STAND" NEAR EACH OTHER—BUT NEITHER TAKES THE GOLD!

Do you want to talk about the good things in life? Read on!

The Public Broadcast System in the United States produced a TV series called "Made in America." The official sourcebook for the series was called *Where We Stand*. It looked at thousands of things people do everywhere in the world, and ranked them.

Rankings were made for seven categories of activities. An addition (mine) of the points for each of the categories was used to establish the overall index. Canada ranked fifth and the United States sixth overall.

The rankings by category indicated that Canada came out ahead of the United States in five of seven categories, but neither country ended up in top spot in any of the categories. Close, but no gold medal!

Canada managed to rank fourth in both the "wealthiest" and "freest" categories. Americans ranked second and third for being the "busiest" and the "smartest."

THE WHERE-WE-STAND INDEX
(ranking among 22 industrial countries)

	Canada	United States	Best
The Wealthiest (affluence):	4	5	Germany
The Smartest (education):	5	3	Germany
The Healthiest (health/ medical advance):	8	12	Japan
The Busiest (productivity):	5	2	Germany
The Freest (open/democratic):	4	13	Australia
The Best Lovers (tolerant/loving):	9	10	Netherlands
The Best Home (habitable):	14	17	Japan
OVERALL	5	6	Japan

Source: Michael Wolff, *Where We Stand.* New York: Bantam Books, 1992.

85/AMERICANS ARE BETTER PREPARED TO COMPETE GLOBALLY

Canada's overall competitiveness is dropping while the United States is now in top spot.

The World Economic Forum has been publishing competitiveness reports since 1980. Their rankings are based on statistical indicators of competitiveness as recorded by international organizations and on perceptions of business executives regarding the competitiveness of their respective countries.

The 1994 report suggests that the U.S. is the most competitive country in the world followed by the Singapore. The U.S. recovered from fifth spot two years ago. Canada slid to 16th position. Canada had ranked fourth and fifth during the early 1990s.

The United States now ranks first in terms of domestic economic strength, internationalization and finance. Canada's best rankings relate to finance and infrastructure.

The survey of business executives is not as favourable to either country with rankings of 10 and 19 for the United States and Canada respectively.

WORLD ECONOMIC FORUM WORLD COMPETITIVENESS: RANKINGS – 1993

	Canada	United States	Best
Overall ranking:	16	1	United States
Factors of competitiveness:			
-Domestic economic strength	15	1	United States
-Internationalization	19	1	United States
-Government	22	6	Singapore
-Finance	8	1	United States
-Infrastructure	2	3	Norway
-Management	19	5	Japan
-Science and technology	19	2	Japan
-People	11	6	Singapore
Executive opinion survey	19	10	Singapore

Source: World Economic Forum, *The World Competitiveness Report 1994,* Geneva.

PART 16

*AND
IN
CONCLUSION...*

"DIFFERENT ENOUGH"

In the past, the "old tape" kept repeating that "Canadians and Americans are the same." It kept repeating that "the rule of 10:1" works, and that Canada was a mini-U.S.A.

Now, a "new tape" (also available in CD) has been edited and updated. It will now repeat that Canadians and Americans are "different enough." And, the "rule of 10:1" does not work often enough to apply.

Borderlines has summarized many significant differences between Canadians and Americans; some are favourable and some are not. A few of the differences are listed here.

Canadians

- are more likely to be Catholics than Protestants
- live further east on the continent
- are outnumbered by Californians
- are less likely to live in metropolitan areas
- don't like Americans as much as Americans say they like Canadians
- think Americans are snobs, whereas Americans think Canadians are nice
- don't want to be part of the United States
- are more likely to think they are essentially different from Americans
- know a lot about America whereas Americans know little about Canada
- are less proud of their country
- are much more likely to vote
- don't believe in the devil and hell as much as Americans do
- are more accepting of sexual freedom
- are increasing their life expectancy relative to Americans
- are having fewer babies
- are waiting longer to have babies
- are having fewer abortions

- are taking in many more immigrants relative to total population.
- are aging faster
- can say that women outnumber men to a lesser extent than do American women
- are less likely to divorce
- can say that women stay divorced longer than American women do
- are more likely to cohabitate for larger periods
- have created fewer jobs
- have more self-employment
- do less moonlighting
- are now more likely to be unemployed
- pay more taxes
- have less personal debt
- have less income inequality
- have fewer children that live in poverty
- eat out less
- spend less on health-care
- like their health care system much more
- have more freezers
- have fewer murders
- can say that violent crime is growing faster in Canada
- are happier
- rank number one on the United Nations Human Development Index
- rank lower on the competitiveness index

Canadian and American similarities are also evident:
- have diverse populations
- populations are shifting west
- populations are growing fastest in metropolitan areas
- see the other people as equally attractive
- have majorities who think Canadians and Americans are the same
- think the same way on the majority of social issues
- have little faith in their institutions
- have similar attitudes on abortion
- believe women don't get as good a deal as men
- smoke at the same rate
- are living longer
- populations are aging
- have more remarriages as a share of all marriages
- have the same number of years of divorce for men
- spend about the same amount on education
- rank poorly on educational assessments
- benefit from education
- have rapid female labour force expansions
- have the same ratio of part-timers

- have rising service employment
- don't go to public employment agencies
- have flat family incomes
- have women closing the income gap
- have homes filled with gadgets
- have large groups that are disadvantaged
- rank high in some international rankings
- are happy with life compared to most other countries

The lists could go on and on...

These comparisons suggest that Canadians and Americans are, on balance, "different enough"—and Canadians want to keep it that way. Canadians want to keep it that way even if Canadians do not openly express the depth of pride and satisfaction in their country that Americans are more prone to do.

Canadians are "different enough"—but most Canadians want to have an open relationship with the United States and its people. Americans are not only our neighbours; they are also our "friends." Canadians want to be separate, but together within North American. Canadians want their friends to know and understand them better.

Former Canadian prime minister Lester B. Pearson, when asked if he was an American, expressed his Canadianism by answering "Yes, I am a Canadian." Likewise, Arthur Phelps, a Canadian writer and speaker, said that "A Canadian is [someone] who has become North American without becoming an American."

86/I WANT CANADA

I want Canada's future to continue to be a caring and kind place. I want a Canada where people come first. I want a friendly country where a mix of individualism and community are combined to build a "nice" country in which to live and work. I want a Canada that accepts change and makes tough choices in a difficult financial environment. I want a Canada that preserves the best of the past, cherishes the present, and focuses on the challenges of the future. I want a country that can improve its competitive base. I want a distinctive Quebec to be part of Canada. I want Canadians to be friends with Americans. That is the Canada in which I want to live in the future. I want to continue to be be *"different enough."*

I like the United States, but I *love* Canada.

ABOUT THE AUTHOR

Roger Sauvé is a futurist, economist, demographer, corporate planner and part-time journalist who has studied households and families for over two decades. His first book, *Canadian People Patterns,* was published in 1990. A former president of the Toronto Association of Business Economists, he holds an undergraduate degree in social sciences and a master's in economics. He is a member of the World Future Society.

He has worked with organizations in the oil (Imperial Oil), financial (CIBC), retail (Eaton's), mining (INCO), agri-food (Saskatchewan Wheat Pool), bio-tech, publishing, co-operative and government sectors. He is a frequent speaker and has been interviewed by the print, radio and television medias in both official languages. He has been a regular columnist in two Prairie dailies, and has been published in other journals including *The Financial Post.* He has travelled extensively in Canada, the United States and Europe. Roger Sauvé has lived and worked in Ottawa and Toronto, and now resides in Regina.